INVEST IN LIVING

IMPROVING YOUR KITCHEN

by

AILEEN LEVENE

EP Publishing Limited
1978

The *Invest in Living* Series

All About Herbs
Fruit Growing
Gardening under Protection
Getting the Best from Fish
Getting the Best from Meat
Growing Unusual Vegetables
Home-baked Breads and Scones
Home Decorating
Home Electrical Repairs
Home Energy Saving
Home Furnishing on a Budget
Home Goat Keeping
Home Honey Production
Home-made Butter, Cheese and Yoghurt
Home-made Pickles and Chutneys
Home Maintenance and Outdoor Repairs
Home Plumbing
Home Poultry Keeping
Home Rabbit Keeping
Home Vegetable Production
Home Woodworking
Meat Preserving at Home
101 Wild Plants for the Kitchen
Wild Fruits and Nuts

About the Author

Aileen Levene has had considerable experience in the home field, having been a Home Editor on a well-known practical journal, as well as being a consultant and 'home expert' on a number of do it yourself journals.

The subjects she covers range from advice on interior design matters, through to home planning, general light practical work—from building cupboards to making patios and water gardens—even advice on repairs to buildings, both inside and exterior work.

Her forte is certainly in the home planning sphere, having involved herself in this subject, particularly kitchens, when on the practical journals, *Do It Yourself* magazine, *Golden Homes, Practical Home Building and Decorating.*

With two kitchens of her own behind her—she re-designed and constructed them practically from scratch—Aileen Levene is well aware of the mistakes and successes that a major improvement involves, and has imparted this knowledge in the book so that it may be of practical use to others who are determined to improve their kitchens and so realise a dream.

Acknowledgements

The author wishes to thank the following for their co-operation and help in writing this book:

Atag, The Building Centre Group, Dunlop Semtex Ltd, The Electrical Association for Women, The Electricity Council, English Rose Kitchens Ltd, The Gas Council, Hygena Ltd, GEC/Xpelair, The Institute of Plumbing, Di Lusso Kitchens Ltd, Magnet & Southerns Ltd, Miele Ltd, Nairn Floors Ltd, Schreiber Furniture Ltd, National Home Improvement Council, Solarbo Fitments Ltd, Thorn/Moffat Ltd, TI Industries Ltd, Wrighton Ltd.

The publishers wish to thank Dunlop Semtex Limited for providing the front cover illustration which shows a country-type kitchen which was once a scullery; the company's vinyl floor tiles are used for the floor.

Contents

Introduction

Is your kitchen well planned, practical and pleasant to work in? Hazarding a guess the probable answer in most cases is 'no'. The average kitchen is small, ill-lit and badly ventilated having evolved into a work centre consisting of a haphazard arrangement of storage units and necessary equipment like the sink, cooker and minimal working surfaces.

Well perhaps in decades past the fact that the kitchen was not functioning well meant simply putting up with the situation. But there is no reason why any self-respecting cook should 'soldier on' in awkward conditions in this labour-saving age.

Today we are fortunate that at our fingertips and within even the humblest budgets there are appliances, kitchen accessories and units available which can turn an unexciting working area into something approaching a dream kitchen.

No, this is not pie-in-the-sky but fact—particularly now when every penny counts both up and down the social scale. It is amazing what can be achieved by simply applying common sense with a fair seasoning of imagination to basic planning principles and, voilà, the results can be gratifying.

There are, of course, certain rules one has to consider and bearing in mind that what suits one does not necessarily suit another, a good, working kitchen is well within everyone's reach.

The basics of good kitchen design have been known for centuries. The Romans, for example, were some of the first to introduce well planned, civilised kitchens which incorporated grills, roasting and warming ovens, sinks and work surfaces as well as cooking utensils and implements.

Nowadays it is a different story—kitchens do not now have to cope with feeding legions, instead just the general requirements of a 'family' so that the needs of the individual family should apply to the kitchen layout.

No other room in the house needs more careful planning and, in a sense, furnishing. At the same time, in no other room will errors in layout and fitting of units or equipment show up so clearly. By the same token—as cooks through the ages have known—the arrangement of appliances and of kitchen storage can make a tremendous difference to how hard the cook has to work. It is quite possible to design a kitchen that will completely exhaust the most durable cook! So do not take your kitchen planning too lightly or hurriedly or you will perhaps find yourself getting in your own way; by careful thought costly mistakes can be avoided.

Planning a scheme

Planning a scheme is not as difficult as one might imagine. Your layout should allow for your not having to make a single unnecessary movement. This is very important for, on average, a housewife spends up to eight hours a day working in the kitchen and travels up to nearly three miles while doing so. Remember each movement counts, from bending down to stretching upwards when putting things away in cupboards. A good plan covers all contingencies.

Meeting your needs
It is important to decide whether the kitchen you have meets your own personal requirements—you may be a meticulous, efficient cook who can produce miracles in the kitchen—so everything must be within fingertip reach. Alternatively, you may feel that because you spend so much time in the kitchen it becomes a part of the integral living area, providing services for the family other than just a place to prepare food.

Be logical, adopt a commonsense approach and appraise your situation—bearing the following factors in mind.

1. Consider the size of your family and its general living habits. This is essential in assessing how the kitchen is used and how much storage space and clear area you will need.
2. Do you eat in the kitchen as a family? Just snacks or full meals? Do children and toddlers, only, eat in the kitchen—and do the latter play there too?
3. Do you entertain your friends in the kitchen? Some people like company when they are working in the kitchen, so a place for folks to sit is useful.
4. Do you keep cleaning equipment like vacuum cleaners, brooms and mops in the kitchen? Also, do you wash clothes and iron them in the kitchen?
5. List the essential major appliances you have, like sink (or sink unit), cooker, refrigerator, washing machine and so on. Then list those you would like to include—a dishwasher, perhaps, maybe a freezer or, possibly, a split level cooker.

Work centres
Having sorted out the factors for your personal kitchen blueprint, the next step is to consider where the main centres of activity should be, so that work flows smoothly from the moment you have unpacked your shopping bag to the moment dinner is ready to be served.

Over many years, considerable research has been carried out to establish optimum working conditions for kitchen users. Gradually as appliances and equipment have become more streamlined and sophisticated, and storage units have improved in design and function, so the results of the researches are a set of clear and easily applied guide lines for averaging out working surface heights, reasonable distances to be covered when doing various kitchen jobs, and suggesting what should be put next to what for work to flow smoothly and for the kitchen to work for you.

In effect it has been found that there are three major work centres within any kitchen plan.

They are: food storage—for storing perishable and non-perishable foods; a sink—for providing water and drainage; and cooking facilities—to provide heat for cooking.

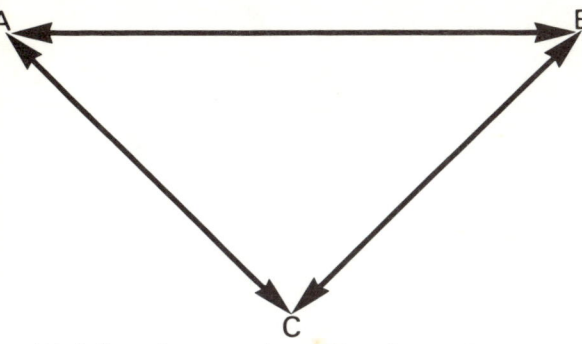

Work flow diagram – the walking distance between all the main work areas should not be more than 6 m (20 ft)
A Goods storage/mixing on worktop
B Sink, worktop/serving   C Cooking area

These three areas form a working triangle linked with secondary areas—working surfaces and general cupboard and drawer space. Ideally they should be positioned about 1200 to 1800 mm (4 ft to 6 ft) apart. The total walking distance between sink, cooker and food preparation/storage centres should be no more than 6 m (20 ft).

Also, each of the zones should have a working surface on either side to speed up the operating sequence. For example, near the refrigerator or larder, where the perishables are kept, there should be a worktop where the shopping bag is unloaded and items immediately put away. The sink area—incidentally the busiest of the three centres—needs a working surface on which vegetables and foods can be prepared ready for cooking, where utensils and crocks can be stacked for washing and draining. This can be a large draining board or a drainer plus an extra working surface.

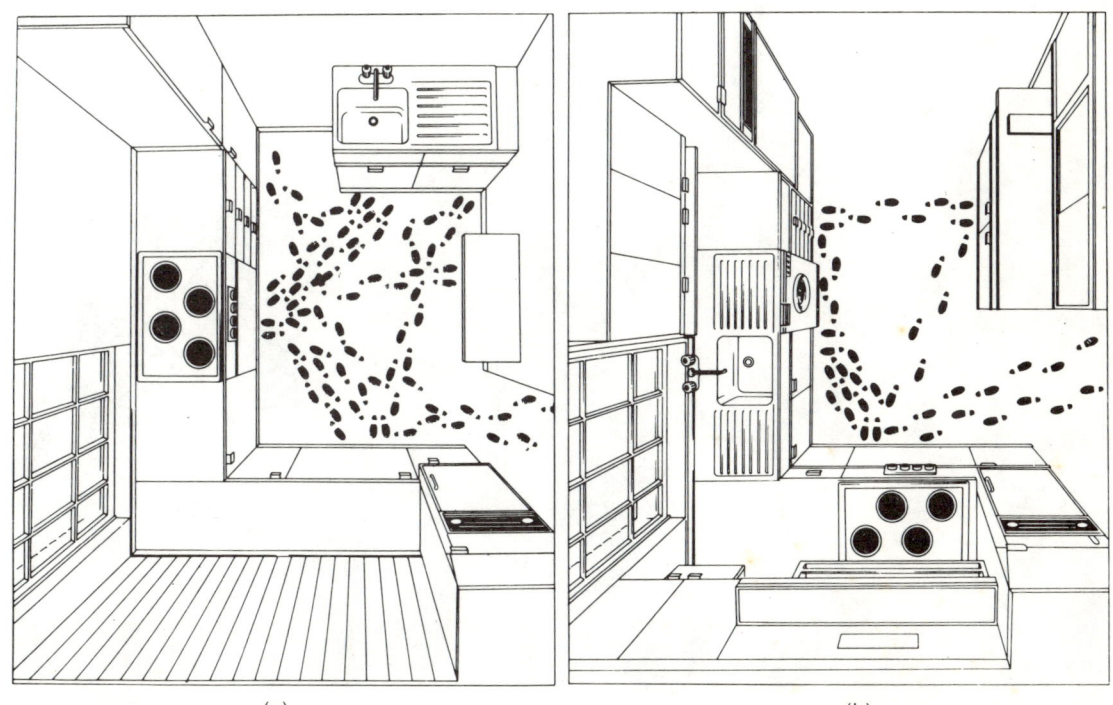

(a)   (b)

Working patterns—turning wasted effort (a) into a reasonable work pattern (b)

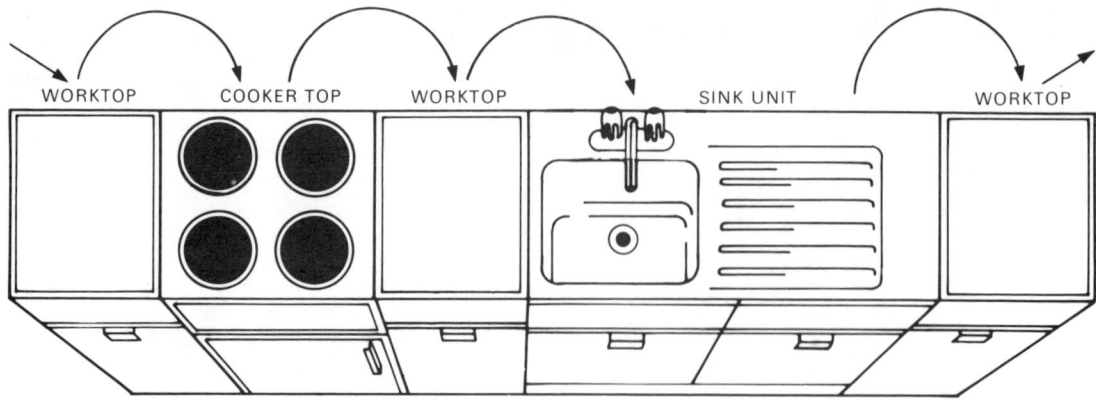

The perfect working arrangement—worktop, cooker hob, worktop, sink unit, worktop

English Rose's 'Infinite' range is seen in this kitchen. The unusual rattan fronts are protected by wipe-clean acrylic sheets. The arrangement here provides a virtually perfect working sequence of operations

The cooker centre—and this applies to a single cooker or a separate oven and hob—should also have a working surface on either side. This is where foods are mixed for cooking and serving, and for setting down hot pans and dishes. Here, particularly, the working surfaces should be heat resistant.

Fining down

Let's look at these areas more closely and see what else should be necessary.

For example, near the larder or fridge it makes sense to keep a cupboard or drawers to hold the ubiquitous silver foil, sealing film, polythene bags and greaseproof paper, plastic airtight food containers, plus the other paraphernalia used to wrap and store foods prior to being put away.

The preparation area, a general purpose one, needs quite a lengthy working surface, near which are bowls, plates, pots and pans, kitchen tools and gadgets.

In the sink area must be adequate space for detergent, cleaning materials, bowls, cloths, mops and so forth. This is the busiest of all the working centres so its positioning is vital. And, its position will automatically dictate where the other two work centres will go.

Near the cooking area should be all the kitchen tools and utensils, seasonings, herbs, baking trays and so forth.

If laundry is carried out in the kitchen, this in effect acts as a separate work centre too.

So, armed with some basic planning considerations, it is time to draw up a plan of your existing kitchen to see whether or not, by juggling with the layout, it will meet a new, easier working sequence or need to be completely remodelled.

Planning and selecting the layout

How to realise your tailor-made kitchen is next. There are no magic wands to wave here; instead you have to work at it for some time so allow plenty of time to reach a satisfactory working arrangement which suits your ideas as well as your pocket.

Now we are officially metric, old British Imperial measures no longer applies—calculate measurements in metric units, preferably millimetres (mm) and metres (m). As furniture is now made to metric modules allow for this when you draw-up your plan.

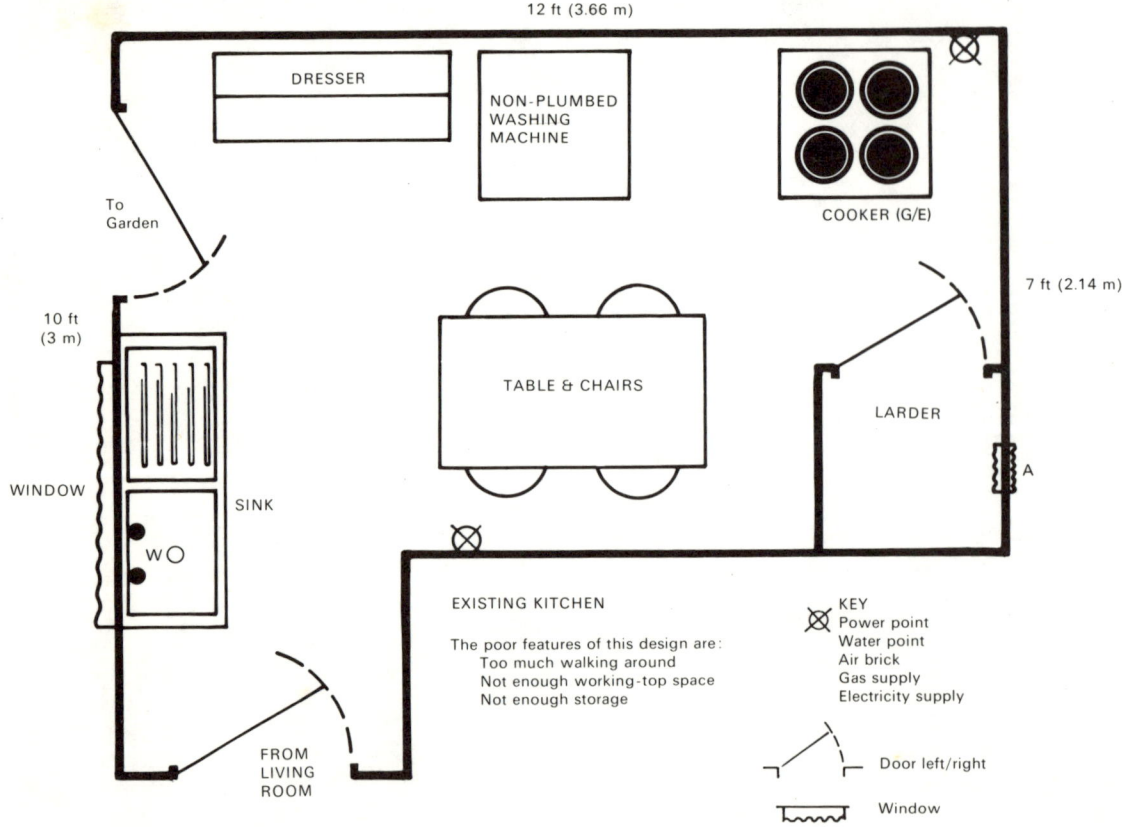

Plan of an existing, inadequate kitchen to be redesigned

It is easier if you do your scale drawing to a metric measure, but if you use a steel rule which incorporates both metric and Imperial units, you will find this helps you to identify the area measurements—especially if you are unfamiliar with using metric measure.

First step

What you need are sheets of graph paper; large sheets of squared paper to allow you to work things out to scale. Use paper which has, say ten small squares for every 10 mm or 1 in, this will make scale drawing relatively painless.

1. Now select your scale, say five small squares which represent 100 mm or 1 ft. If your existing kitchen is 3 m by 3.66 m (10 ft by 12 ft), the floor plan's basic outline will only measure 150 mm by 183 mm (5 in by 6 in).

2. It is important to remember, too, that you may need to mark on your plan a lot of additional and useful information. Therefore your basic floor plan should not occupy the whole sheet, so allow for this by using a fairly large sheet of paper—it can always be trimmed.

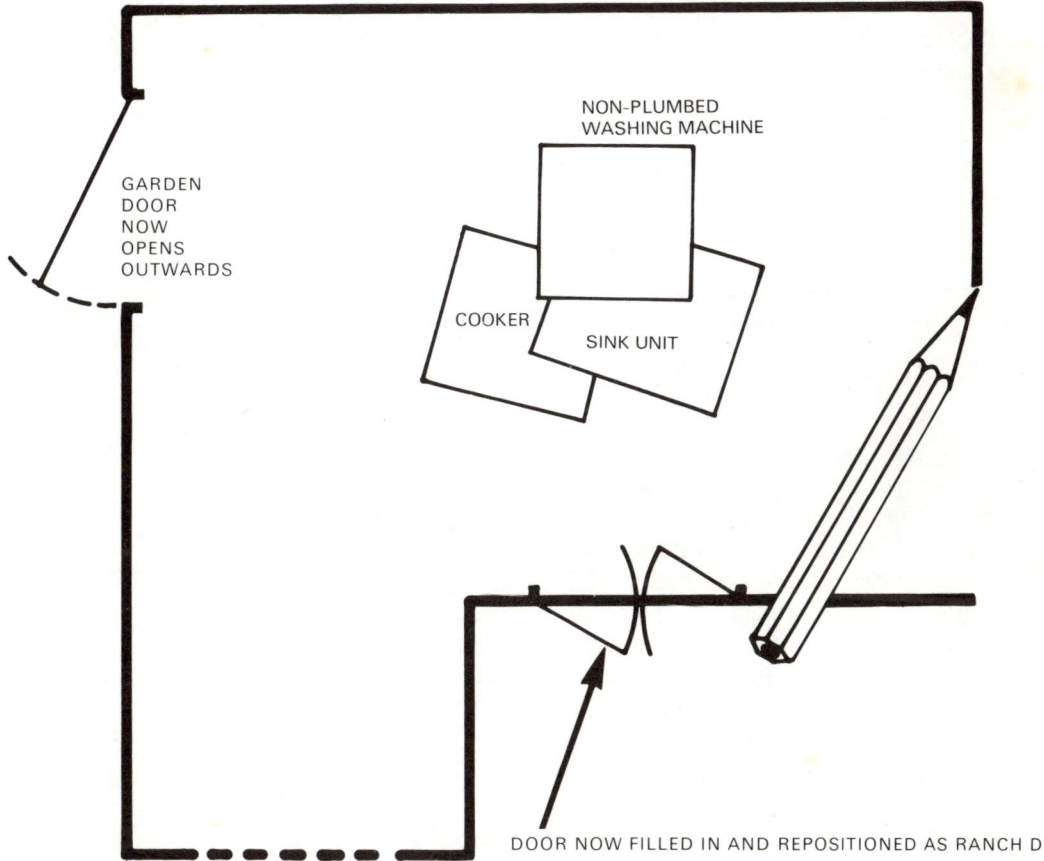

GARDEN
DOOR
NOW
OPENS
OUTWARDS

NON-PLUMBED
WASHING MACHINE

COOKER

SINK UNIT

DOOR NOW FILLED IN AND REPOSITIONED AS RANCH DOORS

With your outline clear of any appliances, you can then move your scale cut-outs around to try out potential new arrangements

3. When measuring windows and doorways, height and depth as well as position, you should include the frames and mouldings within these measurements.

   It is also worth considering, when you are measuring up, that if you leave the existing skirting board in place, any kitchen units you put in may have to be cut away to fit. However, if the skirting board is removed, units can be butt-fitted against the wall, and no alterations need be made to them.

4. Next, check your opposite wall-length measurements to ensure that they match up. Small inaccuracies soon mount up and complicate planning when it comes to choosing furniture or equipment for a critically close fit.

   Carry out frequent spot checks on your measurements across from wall to wall, as opposite walls are often not parallel. This will definitely affect your flooring calculations and could result in an awkward gap behind a long line of rigid units, which will need filling.

5. On your plan do not forget to include things like pipe runs, radiators, plumbing fixtures like stopcocks, air bricks, gas and electric points, meters (frequently located in kitchen larders—these may have to be re-sited). Use different coloured inks for coding these obstructions with appropriate symbols.

6. If a major alteration of the kitchen is on the cards, why not draw two basic layouts? Plan 1 will show your new kitchen with anticipated alterations, with Plan 2 showing the basic outline. (Obviously Plan 1 is useless if you decide the alterations are not possible from a practical or a budget point of view.)

7. Now, incorporate your existing appliances and equipment on the plan, together with measurements of proposed additional equipment you want to buy.

   This also applies to any existing furniture—like tables and chairs or stools—and cupboards. So make some scale cut-outs to make their placing easier.

8. It is a fairly simple job. Once again, use graph paper which you glue down onto thin card and then draw out the length and width (front to back) of every piece of existing equipment plus, as suggested, proposed new things (specifications are supped on manufacturers' brochures).

   Where cupboard doors open out and fitments have drawers, it is worth noting this—either by dotting or with an arrow—or perhaps by drawing out the extra space needed and bending this area up as a flap. This will remind you not to put doors at right angles to each other as they will probably interlock or, perhaps, open the wrong way at corners!

   Write in on each piece the length by width by height (and always in that order, so the height figure is always last), then cut out each piece.

   Now you have a permanent record of each piece of equipment/appliance/furniture which you can then easily move around on your prepared plan, just like pieces in a jig-saw puzzle. This flexibility of switching and swopping helps one to visualise the kitchen as a whole.

   In front of you now is a record showing you exactly what space there is and where it is—in fact, everything is accounted for down to the last piece of equipment.

So armed with your basic working plan your next important step is towards deciding on your own personal working layout.

Basic shapes

The well designed kitchen usually conforms to one of six basic layouts:
1. The one-wall 'single line' kitchen
2. The parallel or galley kitchen
3. The U-shaped kitchen
4. The L-shaped kitchen
5. The F-shaped kitchen
6. The island site kitchen.

Of course the kitchens of today offer a tremendous range of permutations with the various appliances and units now made. However, all of them are eventually reduced down to a variation of one of six fundamental shapes.

Single line kitchen

Perhaps this is the simplest kitchen arrangement for narrow areas like corridors. The plan can allow for windows (if there are any); and usually shows doors at each end of the kitchen space.

By the way if there are no windows in this area—and this happens frequently in flats or bed-sits—then it is essential that good permanent supplementary lighting is installed.

Alternatively, this layout is often the only answer to kitchens in flats, so it means that the cooking area should be screened off by folding or sliding doors, or possibly a free-standing room divider.

The work pattern adopted here is a fairly simple one, but can involve a lot of walking—remember the total walking distance between sink, cooker and food preparation/storage should not be beyond 6 m (20 ft).

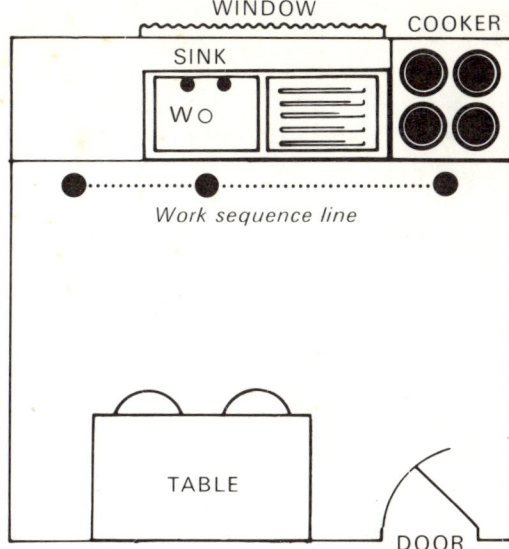

A 'single line' kitchen—a one wall arrangement ideal for narrow kitchens, converted sculleries or bed sits

The limiting factor here, however, is that traffic is liable to flow through the working area causing some inconvenience.

Parallel or Galley kitchen

Similar in many ways to the single line

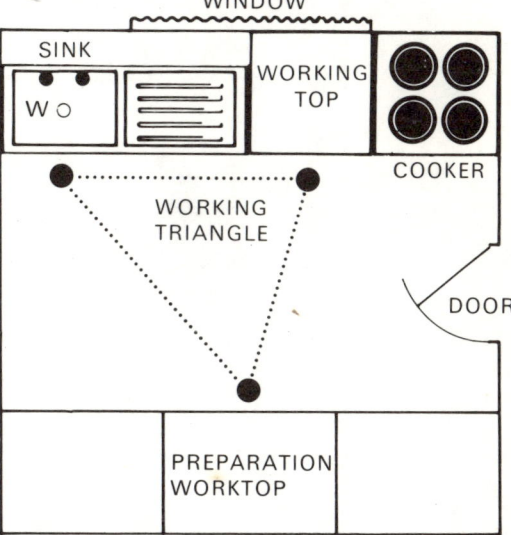

A parallel or galley layout
You see two parallel runs here, with the cooker and sink on one side of the kitchen, food preparation and storage on the other

kitchen it is usually found in long, narrow areas like converted scullery/morning rooms or even passageways, generally found in older houses.

The ideal to aim for here would be for all the large equipment, food storage and preparation area be located on one side, with a continuous work surface, incorporating the cooker and sink on the other.

Remember that you need at least 1200 mm (4 ft) between the two rows as a safe passageway.

Once again, the possibility of constant traffic disturbing you while working is the minus factor for this layout.

In some cases it may be possible to move or relocate one of the doors to a side wall, this allows more planning scope through breaking up the parallel lines.

The U-shaped kitchen

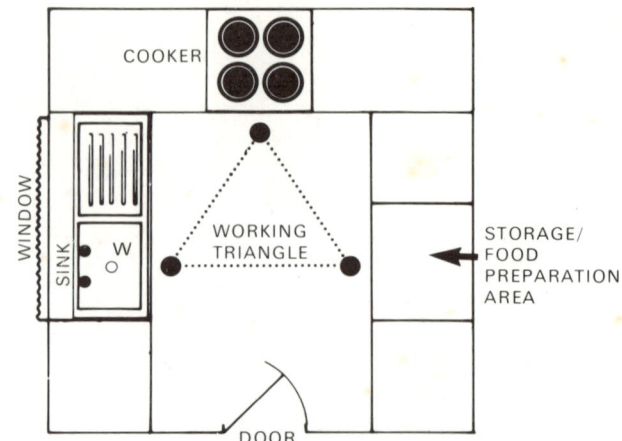

A U-shaped kitchen—where the working sequence is virtually wrapped around the kitchen's walls—ideal for a small kitchen

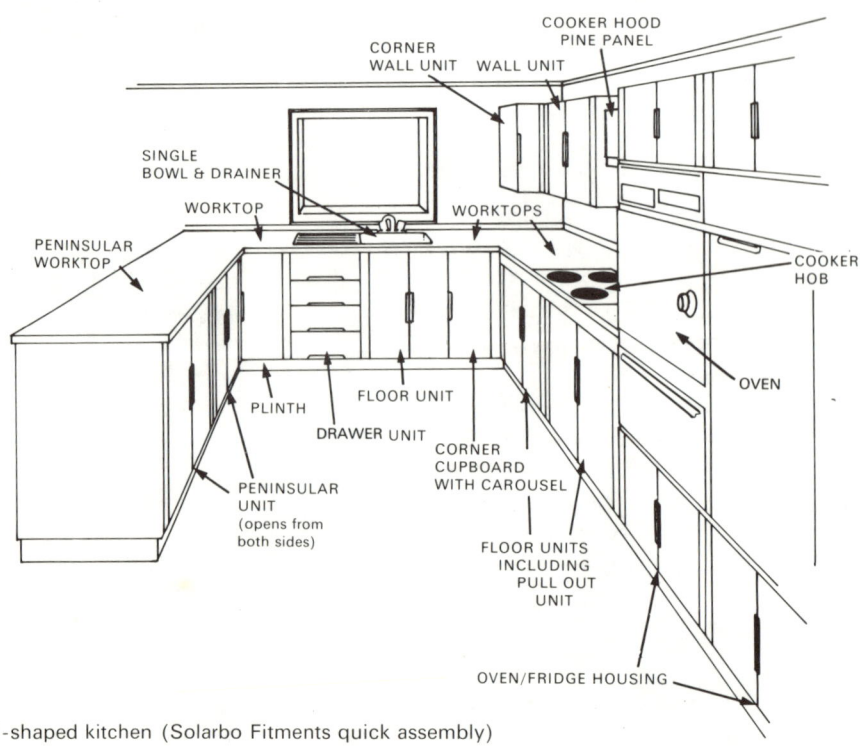

A typical U-shaped kitchen (Solarbo Fitments quick assembly)

This is a very adaptable layout; its compact formation is convenient, as all working areas are within easy reach. It provides a lot of working surface as well as the possibility of wall storage, window area permitting. However, bear in mind your budget, as you will use more cupboards going round two corners.

As a working layout it is often the only choice for small kitchens or in kitchens where eating sections as well as doorway areas are confined to the corners at one end of the room.

In a large kitchen, one leg of the 'U' might well be a peninsular unit top, or even a breakfast bar. However, work out first that the peninsular unit does not impede your access to doorways, say to the garden or even to the main hall serving the front door, or you will be 'trotting' round it umpteen times a day!

The L-shaped kitchen

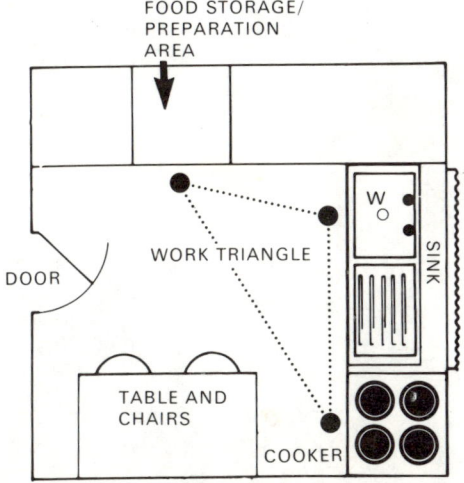

An L-shaped kitchen offers a good basic layout, whose design allows for a natural flow of work

The work sequence here can be arranged in its natural order and the triangle kept compact. It is a good basic layout, lending itself well to both large and small kitchens, for there is a reasonable area for free circulation.

For rooms with difficult shapes—lots of doors and perhaps windows in awkward places—this layout is often the best one to adopt.

Where you have a large area, it is often possible to incorporate a room divider cum breakfast counter, and a work centre for laundry still leaving room for a kitchen table—that maid of all work—in the centre of the room.

The F-shaped kitchen

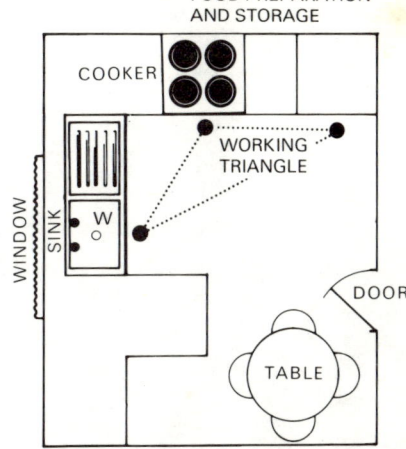

An F-shaped kitchen—really a combined U- and L-shape, which provides considerable worktop and storage space. Particularly useful is the peninsular unit and area beyond for eating/relaxing

This is really a combination of the L- and the U-shapes. The marriage provides much more working surface and room for more appliances. It is an ideal layout with 'adding to' in mind. So you can either start off with an L-shaped or a U-shaped layout and adapt accordingly as and when your budget and needs allow.

The Island layout

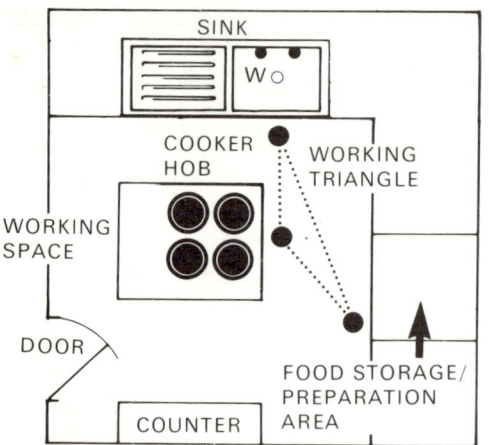

The island layout—often used in conjunction with an L- or U-shaped kitchen with a central bank of built-in worktop and cooker hob. A larger unit can also hold a sink and a small refrigerator. After all, a large table in a kitchen is, in effect, an island unit

Often considered the most *avant-garde* of working centres, this layout normally seems to be associated with large luxury kitchens, but in fact is often the answer to many ordinary kitchen problems.

If you need wall space, or the walls are in bad shape, sloping for example or when the walls include a large number of windows, doors, a central heating boiler or pipework, then an island layout is well worth considering.

Here some of your major appliances are fixed in the centre of the room. When and if you move house the island unit is easy to dismantle.

Remember, also, a large kitchen table used for preparing food effectively becomes an 'island' work centre in relation to the rest of the room.

Island kitchen. **Hygena** 'New 2000' range

Ergonomics in the kitchen

Now let us look at correct working heights of surfaces and appliances.

Life would be much simpler if Mrs Housewife was a standard size in height and reach. Manufacturers of appliances and furniture would be able to cater for their ideal by making all products conform to the set size. But, as we know, this is quite impossible; and adding to the problem is the fact that different jobs need surfaces of varying heights to make sure they are completed comfortably.

Comfort

Comfort is the operative word to bear in mind. It is essential that one has cupboard and work surfaces of the right height and width to avoid unnecessary physical effort and strain while working.

Hygena's 'Montana' self-assembly kitchen units

It is well known that many accidents and ailments are caused by awkward working heights and badly placed storage units and kitchen appliances. In fact there are as many accidents in the kitchen as there are on the roads, which is a staggering thought!

Acceptable comfort levels

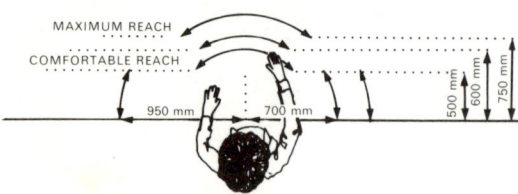

An overhead view of comfortable and maximum reach from a standing position

The estimated correct working heights for the average woman, 1600 mm (5 ft 4 in) tall when working in the kitchen are listed below, and are based on a 'comfortable reach' for most tasks:

1. Height for a top shelf in an un-obstructed wall unit is 1800 mm (5 ft 10 in);
2. Height for a top shelf over a work-top which is usually set back 300 mm (1 ft) is 1700 mm (5 ft 6 in);
3. Height for a general worktop and sink bottom is 810 mm (2 ft 8 in);
4. Height for mixing food, standing, and for eating, sitting on chairs is 710 mm (2 ft 4 in);
5. Height for 'lap' working when sitting is 600 mm (2 ft);
6. Height for chairs, stools and benches is 400 mm (1 ft 4 in);
7. Height for the lowest storage shelf is 250 mm (10 in);

8. Allow a toe recess at the base of any kitchen unit of 75 mm by 75 mm (3 in by 3 in);
9. Depth of worktops is between 460 mm to 760 mm (1 ft 6 in to 2 ft 6 in) although 600 mm (2 ft) is quite adequate;
10. Depth of general storage is 600 mm (2 ft);
11. Depth of china storage is 300 mm (1 ft);
12. Depth of most foodstuffs is 150 mm (6 in).

But even if you are taller or shorter than average (we all vary!) arriving at our correct working levels is not impossible. Inches can be added or removed from base units at the plinth or toe board. Even kitchen table legs can be cut down or raised by blocking. Wall cupboards can be adjusted slightly and so can the shelves inside them. Remember, the effort expended at the 'fitting' stage is well worth the comfort when you are working in the finished kitchen.

A counter height of 900 mm (3 ft) is relatively comfortable for most people, but you can calculate your own best height for comfort by standing up straight in the shoes you normally wear in the kitchen, arms by your sides. Now raise your forearms to bend your elbows. The distance from the floor to your bent elbows less 150 mm to 225 mm (6 in to 9 in) should be the most comfortable counter height for you.

What is advisable is to have two heights of working surface, a slightly lower one for general food preparation and a higher one for the sinktop and draining area. But, you must remember that no difference in height should occur immediately next to a sink bowl or a cooker surface, as this will create

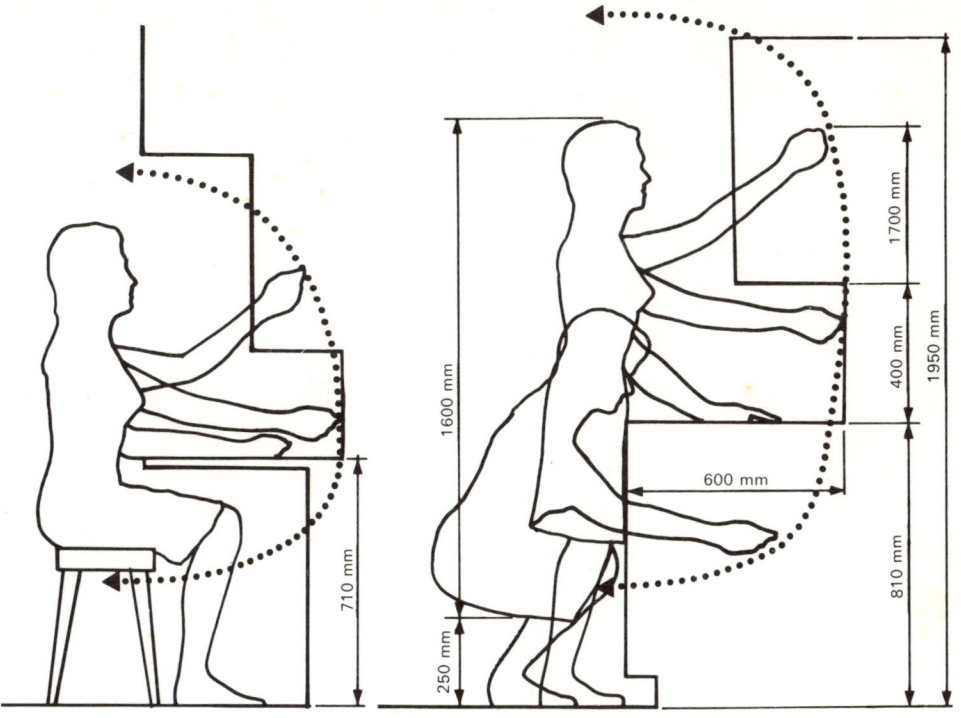

Diagrammatic arrangements based on the comfort reach for easy access of an average woman of 1.6 m (5 ft 4 in) both sitting and standing

an accident zone. A difference in height is easier to introduce at a corner return or as a separate worktop run.

Basic points about safety

At this point in planning, one should consider some of the basic safety aspects in this potentially dangerous area.

Cooker and sink positions

First and foremost your cooker should never be placed opposite your sink. This means that kettles, saucepans, casseroles and hot dishes have to be carried across the kitchen. This must be avoided to prevent serious accidents.

Never put a cooker or hob in front of a window. This can create draughts which could blow out the

gas (if used), upturn pans or perhaps set fire to blinds or curtains.

Hot 'fat flare' from chip and frying pans does often happen and could set curtains or blinds alight. In addition, heat produced by a cooker is considerable and is detrimental to glass.

Electric sockets

Allow sufficient electric sockets on your plan to accept the various appliances you use. It is best to have double switched plugs rather than singles; this eliminates the use of adaptors and overloading of the circuit as well as fuses. The minimum number of sockets in a kitchen is five, but you will probably need more. They should be fixed at a reasonable and easy to reach height and place, to avoid trailing flexes from kettles, mixers and toasters. Remember, if you intend to include new labour-saving devices like cooker hoods, a waste-disposal unit, perhaps eventually a dishwasher and freezer, you must make provision for their electric sockets. It is much easier to do this in the planning stage rather than later, when alterations will disrupt the kitchen and be extremely costly.

There are, of course, many other hazards present in the kitchen. These will be pinpointed in a later chapter with suggestions on how to avoid them.

Practical considerations in your plan

From your scale plan, you can now see that the arrangement of units is dictated by the shape of the room, the position of the windows and doors and certainly, to a degree, the plumbing and other service points.

Take a long look at what you have—is your layout practical? Are you certain you have included everything—all the things you now have plus others you might want in the future?

Analyse each area carefully; it would be a shame to spoil the kitchen for the sake of moving a doorway or, perhaps, opening up a wall to enlarge the area.

Doors

Are there too many doors? If so, would it be practicable to close off any? In some cases a serving hatch could take the place of a spare door allowing you to use the door's 'dead' space for storage.

Alternatively, if your kitchen has a serving hatch plus a door into the dining room, block off the door and turn the hatch into a ranch-style swinging door. This works well but is not a suitable arrangement if there are small childern around.

Move a door from, say, the middle of a wall to the end. This could provide extra storage and work surfaces.

On a more modest scale, simply rehanging a door to open outwards rather than inwards makes a difference.

Larder

That good old-fashioned standby, the larder, is now largely superseded by the refrigerator and occupies precious space. Think hard, do you need it? If not, demolish the larder and utilise its space.

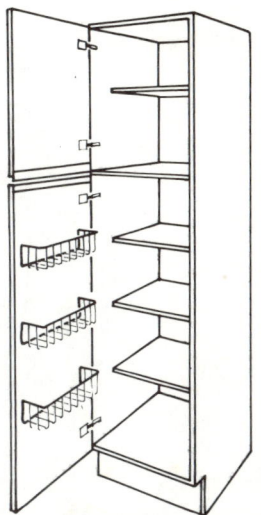

Depending on whether you have extra shelves or not a tall cupboard can act as a broom cupboard or a larder. Do not forget to use the special flex and hose clips shown below to make use of the backs of doors

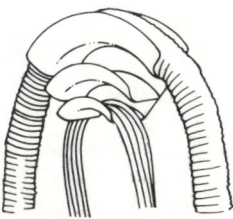

Special moulded nylon clips hold electric flexes and hoses inside broom cupboards

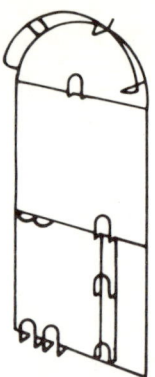

This is a vacuum cleaner accessory rack for fitting in a broom cupboard.

Old fireplaces/boiler cubby holes

Many older houses with sculleries or kitchens have non-functional fireplaces and/or a defunct boiler or copper cubby hole. Why not use this space for a refrigerator or cooker? You can have ventilation through the flue (adapted, of course). Alternatively, seal the flue at ceiling level and open up the chimney breast. Now you have an ideal cupboard and room for shelving in an otherwise lost space.

Windows

Although like doors, too many windows in a kitchen will limit storage space, you do need plenty of natural light.

If you have only one small window, perhaps you can enlarge it. Let in more daylight by glazing a kitchen back door and put in a fixed window light above it.

Nairn 'Cushionflor De Luxe' Jedburgh is on this kitchen floor complementing the Winchmore 'kit kitchen' diy units. Note the clever use of the roller blinds to subdue but not cut out the natural daylight in this busy area

When replacing old casements or sash windows use pivoting picture windows with top lights; this makes window cleaning easier.

If you move your sink position, try and cut in a new window so that you are working in natural light.

Plumbing relocation

Although the position of the sink, washing machine and perhaps, dishwasher, are dependent upon the existing water supply and drainage connections there is no reason to prevent plumbed-in items from being moved around on the plan (but try to keep them to an outside wall to cut down work on drainage). Fortunately today's easily manoeuvrable plastic and copper pipework for plumbing makes this feasible.

If you are getting rid of an old-fashioned boiler system (and hundreds of older houses do still have 'Ideal' kitchen boilers), remember to get rid of the old cast iron pipework, too.

Should the kitchen re-planning coincide with a new central heating system, this could incorporate a wall-hung boiler instead of a floor-standing model; these units can be concealed under the sink or included in a cupboard run, so connections (gas, water and electricity) must be allowed for. Ideally you can site these new compact boilers elsewhere in the house, which would obviate using precious kitchen space. But do remember to allow for some form of background heating in the kitchen, like a free-standing convector heater.

Suspended ceilings

Older houses tend to have lofty ceilings, making lighting inefficient and heating expensive. Why not lower the ceiling, suspending a false one to a reasonable height and incorporate inset lighting? A lower ceiling also means a warmer room where heat is conserved.

A suspended ceiling, for practical purposes, also masks ducting for ventilation to the outside through an air-brick or ventilator as well as allowing easy access for wiring.

Split-level cooking

While calculating what is best for your own working triangle, remember that a split level cooker—oven and separate hob—is extremely versatile and is a flexible twosome for planning. There is more cupboard space available when you site the units where you want them, so allowing you to take advantage of wall and work surface space.

Power supply

An old-fashioned kitchen is bound to need additional power points or might have to be rewired completely. Provide for this on the plan during the alterations stage rather than make do with insufficient sockets in awkward places.

This also applies to gas connections —it is most important to be able to have your cooker or hob where you want them, even if it means fitting a new length of gas pipe.

For lighting, too, you are bound to need new wiring; this will mean chanelling wires into the ceiling and down the walls. Do this before any redecorating or unit fitting, and check that the lights are in the right place— never behind you as you will be working in your own shadow.

Powered appliances

Are you sure you have listed each appliance and kitchen aid? It is amazing how many you may have already as well as those you are planning to buy eventually.

When you calculate how many you might use at the same time you will see how important it is to have sufficient outlets to cope with the demand.

For example, cooker (or separate oven/hob), kettle, percolator, toaster, mixer, liquidiser, iron, small grill. Then there are the big units: refrigerator, washing machine, water heater, central heating boiler—these are only some of the units one uses every day. Even if you know it is going to be months, perhaps years before you have everything you want, still make allowances.

Extensions

If your plan shows insufficient space for a workable kitchen, do not despair, the answer is to consider an extension or a conversion.

This could be achieved by combining the kitchen with an adjoining dining room, scullery and/or passageway to make a larger room, or by building onto the kitchen shell, space permitting.

The former can be quite straightforward, although building regulations may have to be consulted.

The latter may be the only practical way of making a bigger kitchen, and could be a costly exercise. To see whether either moves are feasible, call in your local authority building inspector for his advice and act upon it, accordingly.

A place for everything

What is important in a well-planned kitchen is that everything kept there is conveniently to hand. So plan your storage like a military campaign. Once your work centres have been established tackle storage of food and drinks, utensils, crockery, linen, portable appliances and so on.

The most convenient accessible storage is considered to be between 760 mm (30 in) and 1500 mm (60 in) from the ground. Kept inside this area are the most frequently used items. Below that heavy utensils—pots and pans, mixing bowls, bulk purchases of dry goods, cleaning materials and so on. At a higher level tinned and packaged food is stored together with dishes not used everyday.

What the individual family accumulates in goods and chattels is staggering; apart from normal necessities in food, drink, pots and pans there are all kinds of gadgets and implements which show what type of cook runs the kitchen rather than reflecting the number of people in the family.

Remember, too, if you shop frequently—and most town folk do—your long-term storage needs are bound to be less than your country cousin's; she shops less frequently and so needs more space for her bulk buys.

Be generous with your kitchen storage; allow for the possibility of adding more units as the needs arise.

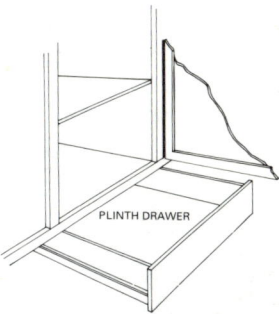

Dead space Often neglected is the space under the 'plinth' at the base of kitchen floor units. Here a drawer has been incorporated—ideal for all those odds and ends one accumulates

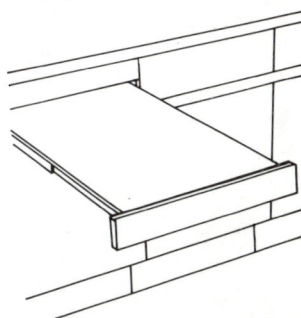

Pull-out flap Additional table space as seen is this flap table top which slides out from underneath the kitchen base unit's working surface

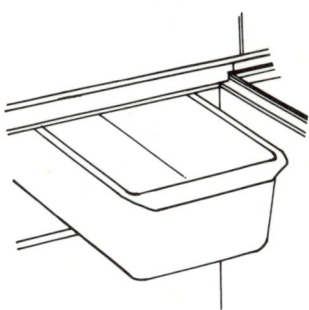

Bread box A bread bin which slides out on runners is useful

Just some of the many types of kitchenware which has to find a home in the normal kitchen

Working to plan

Make a list of all the things you need to keep in the kitchen.

- Food—tinned and packaged, cereals, staples (like tea, sugar, flour), butter, margarine, oil, jars of goods, fresh and frozen meat, vegetables and fish, fruit, condiments, herbs and so forth.
- Crockery—table crockery and cooking crocks like kitchen bowls, casseroles, glassware.
- Cutlery—table cutlery as well as cooking implements, including various knives, choppers, kitchen tools and gadgets.
- Saucepans—general pots and pans, casseroles, baking tins, roasting pans.
- General utensils—sieves, graters, tin openers, bottle openers and so on.
- Kitchen linen—tea towels and hand towels; perhaps place mats, tablecloths and serviettes (if you eat in the kitchen).
- Cleaning materials—various detergents, soap powders, scourers, polishes, cloths and dusters.

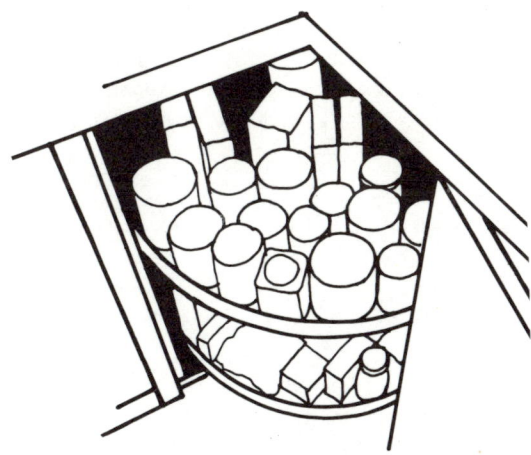

Corner use A corner carousel with 270° storage trays, or a plain shelf can be fitted behind 'swing clear' doors giving direct access

- Cleaning equipment — mops, brooms, dustpans and brushes, vacuum cleaner, perhaps an ironing board, buckets and bowls.
- Small appliances—electric kettles, percolator, toaster, mixer, liquidiser, iron.

What goes where

Now decide where you are going to put your things. Items should be put away where they are most likely to be used, and things used frequently should be closest to hand.

So, ideally, food goes near the preparation area, cooking equipment including utensils between the cooker and sink, and china and cutlery near the sink or eating area.

Do not forget the 'comfort' factor when you fill the shelves and cupboards. The most frequently used items should be within easy arm's reach; heavy items in base units, and less frequently used things in tall cupboards.

Remember, too, that shelves should not be so deep that you cannot reach the back, nor fixed rigid so they cannot be adjusted up or down to take small things like packs of jelly or large items, like giant cereal packets.

Food storage

Your refrigerator is a good friend in the kitchen. It holds most perishable foods, bread and drinks.

With few exceptions, like vegetables—most foods keep well and for long periods if wrapped properly—this prevents dehydration (one of the hazards of keeping foods at low temperatures) and preserves flavours.

If you have no refrigerator then a well-ventilated pantry or larder should be used to keep your perishables cool, but for no more than three days at a maximum. As some larders are not in the kitchen but just outside, it might pay you to invest in a refrigerator which will save your food bills and energy with the inevitable to-ing and fro-ing to take and replace food!

General foods—including tinned, and packaged goods as well as jars of food are usually very heavy and bulky so should be stored in floor cupboards.

But if you use these foods constantly then a wall cupboard should take them. Remember that weight is a crucial factor here, so reinforce the cupboard to prevent distortion, or even the wrenching out of screws from the wall; and reinforce the wall; and reinforce its shelves to prevent their bowing.

Combination storage   A fixed shelf and three wire baskets combine to make the most of cupboard space. Instead of fruit they could hold cleaning materials

Why not store dry goods, like rice, pasta, cereals, vegetables, fruits in screw-topped glass jars; they keep fresh this way and show when they need refilling.

Try to keep your stores regimented in a 'filing' system form. Keep canned vegetables, fish, meat, fruit in rows instead of a haphazard lumping together. Rotate all the things on your shelves, and put new items at the back of each row. As all food deteriorates if kept too long, this is a practical measure.

Frequently used foods—tea, sugar, jam, flour, coffee—are best kept in wall cupboards immediately above or next to the food preparation area.

Herbs, spices and condiments too, should be accessible, preferably near the cooker.

Vegetables must be near the sink for ease of washing and preparation. Keep then in a floor cupboard sitting on plastic covered wire trays allowing the air to circulate. The doors should have vents or mesh inserts to help here. If you prefer to see the vegetables, keep them in well-ventilated vegetable racks in a space between floor units. (You can improvise here by using an office 'beanstalk' with wire mesh trays.)

Crockery

All table crockery, glassware and cutlery are best put near the sink for easy washing up and putting away. Alternatively, if you eat in the kitchen, put them near the eating area.

Excessive loading of wall cupboards is damaging, as already mentioned, and the chief culprit is crockery. Few of us realise that a stack of a dozen dinner plates weighs more than 5.4 kg (12 lb)

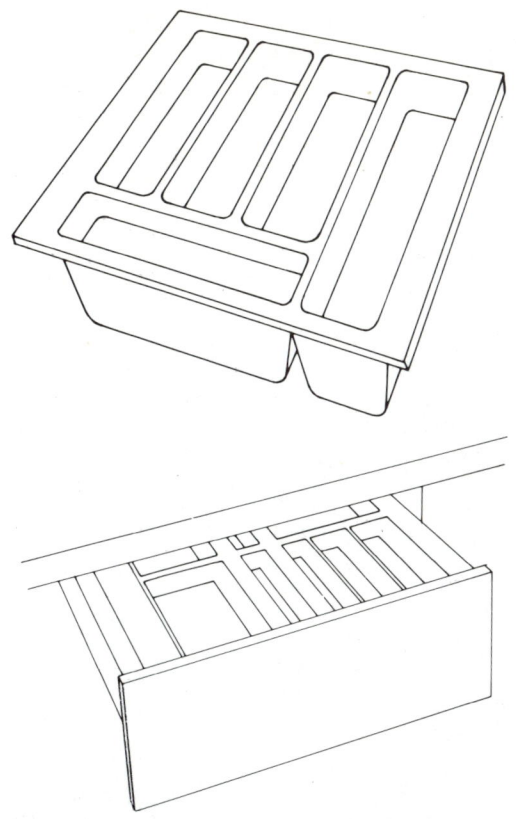

Cutlery trays Available in plastic, these easy-to-clean cutlery trays are light in weight, yet strong and practical

Glassware should be kept on shelves, baize or plastic foam lined, to prevent chipping. Cups should also nestle in clutches of four rather than be hung on hooks, as they gather dust.

Cooking crockery, like mixing bowls, casseroles and serving dishes should be kept as close to the food preparation area as possible, preferably in floor units with drawers to take the accompanying kitchen cutlery.

Why not set aside a 'baking' cupboard, where all articles for the job are together—scales, sieves, mixing bowls, rolling pin, whisks, baking tins?

Frequently used kitchen tools and cutlery can be hung on racks near the cooker above the preparation area. Alternatively, keep them in a deep basket, stoneware jar or wooden box on the working surface.

and side plates, saucers or even soup plates weigh almost as much. Displace the weight evenly by using small piles of plates over a larger area—take up two cupboards for storage instead of one if necessary—and, rather than piling plates use racks.

Space-saving sets of plastic covered wire baskets and acrylic drawers which come with special runners are just right for holding general kitchen items. These take crockery in floor units rather than leaving it to be stacked on shelves. The drawers are very easy to pull out, unload and load.

Heavy items like tinned goods and jars are also easy to store this way.

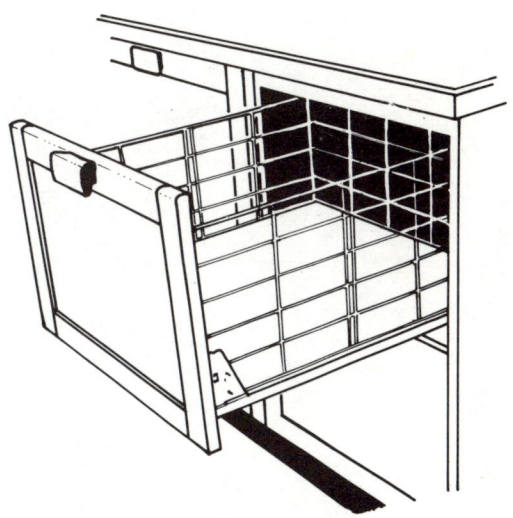

Crockery Always heavy, crockery is ideally stored in strong, pull-out or slide-out drawers or baskets; cooking utensils can also be stored this way

Miele kitchens An under-hob storage unit, the KM14 Hob and Control Unit are also seen, as is the Cooker Hood, DE5

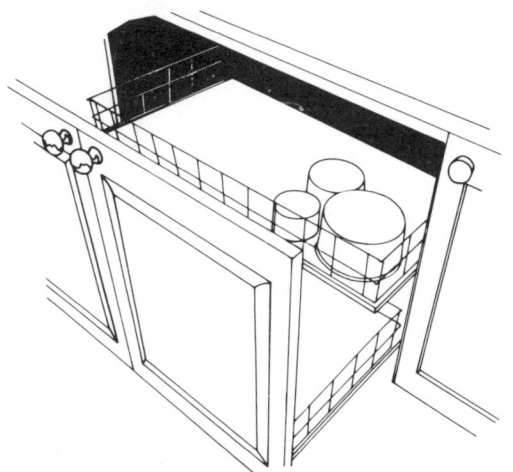

Drawer units Slide-out storage; here is one full shelf and a half shelf for storing different items

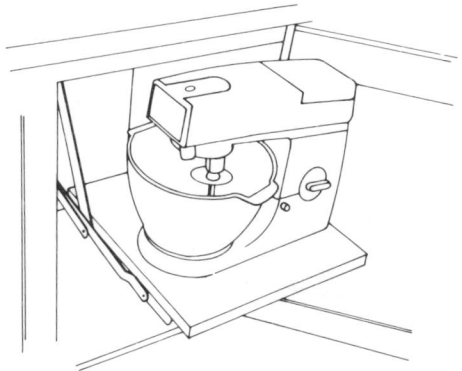

A lifting platform takes the strain out of lifting mixers or other heavy items. The platform is counter-balanced and has storage beneath

Saucepans

Saucepans, frying pans and their lids are space consuming items. Keep them as near to the cooker as possible in floor cupboards, where they can sit tidily one inside the other. Provided they are not too heavy, lids can be hung on the inside of the unit doors either on hooks, or slipped behind securing bars. Or, if you can spare the room, set aside a drawer for the lids alone.

Cleaning materials

All general cleaning items should be kept under the sink secured against prying childrens' fingers. Do not keep volatile items like teak oil, some polishes and other cleaning chemicals there because the space is confined and generally too warm.

Cleaning equipment

Try to keep all cleaning equipment *out* of the kitchen. But if it must live there, then keep the items as far from the food preparation area as possible.

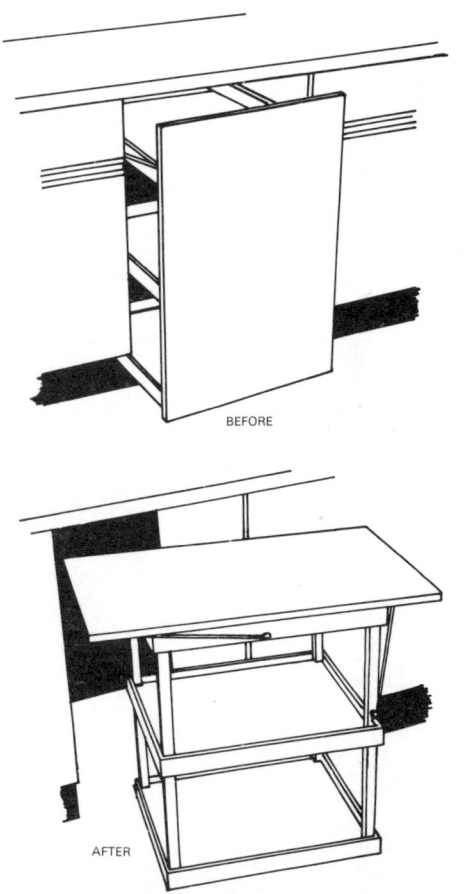

BEFORE

AFTER

Trolley unit This unit pulls out completely to form a two-tier free-standing unit with a laminated top. A clever idea, easily adapted to fit a gap

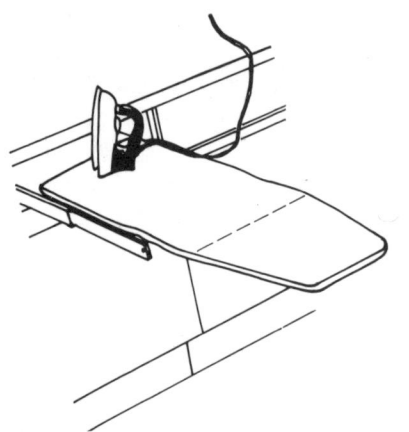

Ironing board A simple idea—slide out your ironing board, unfold it to full length, then sit down to a comfortable session of ironing

Portable appliances

Things like electric kettles, toasters and mixers can live quite happily on worktops as long as at least 500 mm (20 in) space has been allowed between the worktop and the bottom of the wall cupboard for their access.

Oddments

Where there are spaces left under worktops between floor units, use them to hide trays, or tea towels on extending arms. Even a small stool or step ladder to help you reach those tall cupboards can be stored away here.

Wrighton's 'Waltham' range using Pilkington's wall and floor tiles and Creda electric appliances show how the efficient use of storage space will ensure that essential items are easily available

Equipping the kitchen

Because major items of kitchen equipment are expensive to buy and, in some cases, to run, choose them with care. They are going to be with you for some time so, apart from their 'eye appeal' consider their staying power. Also, bear in mind your future needs, so that even if your kitchen plan is re-shuffled in years hence, your equipment will still fit into the scheme of things and continue to serve you well.

Sinks

Let us look at the most used piece of kitchen equipment, the sink.

One is confronted with a tremendous variety of sinks in different sizes, depths and materials. They generally are of two kinds—the integral sink top with drainer, and the inset bowl, or inset bowl with drainer, which is set directly into the working top.

1. Vitreous enamel—your choice can be vitreous enamel with a toughened surface which avoids chipping and scratching and is acid and heat resistant. This type is made in an extremely wide colour range, which means you can match your sink colour to the general kitchen decor. Apart from various sizes there are different shapes, from rectangular to circular bowls, some made particularly shallow specifically for preparing and rinsing vegetables, or for draining dishes.

2. Ceramic sinks—these are still made, but are no longer commonly used in the kitchen.

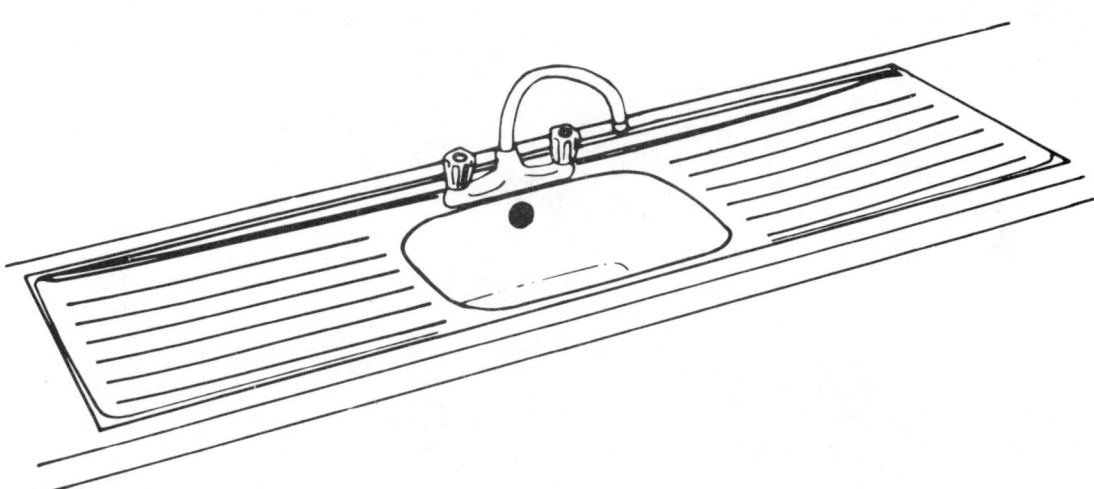

Sinks   An example of a double drainer, single bowl inset sink in a pre-formed plastic laminate worktop

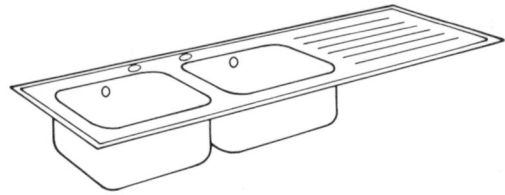

A double bowl single drainer unit, without upstand at the back

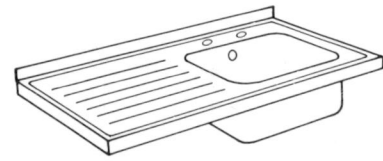

This is a 'sit-on' sink top, single bowl, single drainer, with an upstand at the back. The sink has to line up with the unit on which it sits

3. Stainless steel—has now virtually superseded all other materials for making sinks. Virtually indestructible, it does not chip, nor rust and if scratched, can be polished back to a pristine finish. Some stainless steel sinks are shiny, others are satin finished. The satin process resists scratching and discolouration by surface grease. All sinks clean easily with mild washing-up detergent or non-abrasive cream cleaners.

The combination of bowls and drainers is considerable, so your choice should easily be met.

One is always governed by space in the kitchen and for the average home a one-bowl with drainer sink is the norm. However, in the busy kitchen,

Atag model 86.235 E twin circular sinks inset into worktop

one bowl is really not enough. If you can, install a double sink and a draining board. This at least will help you whizz through the washing-up—wash, rinse and drain pattern. When preparing food, you could be soaking vegetables in one sink, while the other is free for general duties.

Certainly if you shop around you can find small double-bowled sinks which take up only a little more space than the conventional single sink.

Drainers come either right- or left-handed, with or without up-stands. Bowls come with drain outlets either incorporating a cut-out for waste-disposal units or with standard drain outlets.

If you would like a waste-disposal unit put in eventually but initially cannot afford it, the sink with the outlet already cut out can be used by incorporating a removable strainer/waste basket which is an ideal sink tidy.

However, most drain outlets can be cut to take a disposal unit when it is needed.

Inset bowls can come with a drainer sealed into a worktop or without a drainer. Do remember to mop up any water which tends to stay round the sealed edge of the bowl. And for non-standard lengths of worktop, there are some companies which can provide an insetting service. Alternatively, a proficient handyman can cut out a working surface, set in the bowl and seal—and providing an efficient seal is the most important part—to prevent water seepage and dirt being trapped.

When your sink is not in use, a removable cover—like a chopping board—which fits over the bowl will increase your working surface area.

Do not forget that the correct height for your sink is important for easy working. The bottom of the bowl should be the same height as your general working top surface, 810 mm (2 ft 8 in).

Taps

Taps A pillar tap, with a clear acrylic head (this does not get hot to the touch)

A dual-flow type of tap, with swivel spout and clear acrylic head

Another form of pillar tap in IMI polyacetal, white not metallic

A dual-flow tap also in IMI polyacetal, with swivel centre spout; white or brown body

Part and parcel of every sink is the necessary pair of taps, and the market abounds with them from single pillars to mixer units. Whichever you use, make sure they are easy to turn—lever types are very easy—and that washer replacement will not mean a major job.

If you cannot afford a brand new pair of kitchen taps, there are sets of tap-top conversion kits available, too.

Waste-disposal units

Fast shrugging off its 'luxury' image is the waste-disposal unit. It is invaluable in the kitchen as it cuts down on handling some 20 per cent or so unhygienic kitchen waste and slops. The offending rubbish is simply ground up and rinsed away simultaneously down the sink, rather than being put into plastic bags or refuse bins prior to the dustman calling.

Installation is relatively easy, but if in doubt, call in a plumber or builder to advise on the suitability of the existing drains to carry this type of liquid waste.

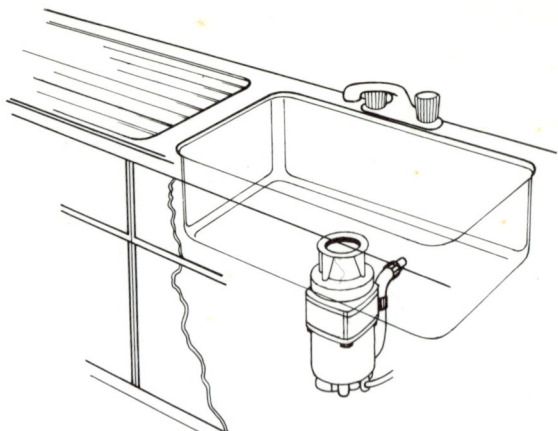

A waste disposal unit fits neatly under the sink

Cookers

Your personal preference for either gas or electricity is the deciding factor, followed by the cost, and the size and shape of the kitchen.

Whichever fuel you prefer to use, there are hundreds of cookers to choose from, each with advantages to offer. Some prefer using gas because of its heat flexibility and easily adjusted

Xpelair Pelican Popular One of the economically priced food waste-disposal units for use in domestic kitchens

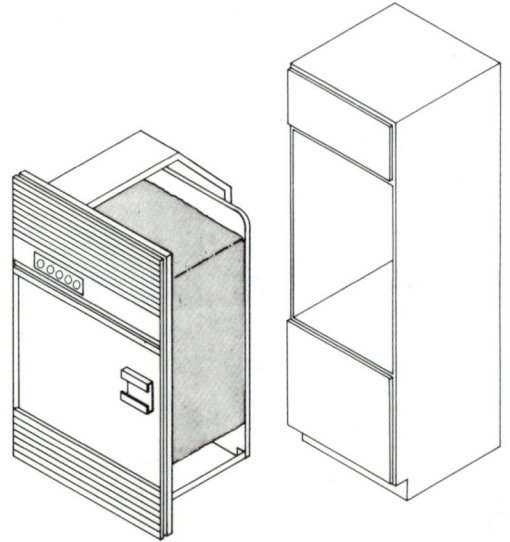

Built-in ovens Built-in oven, this is a Cannon gas-fired oven; side view of appliance and the housing it can fit into

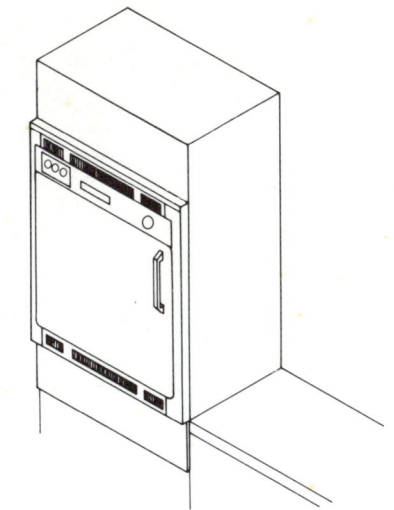

Another gas-fired built-in oven

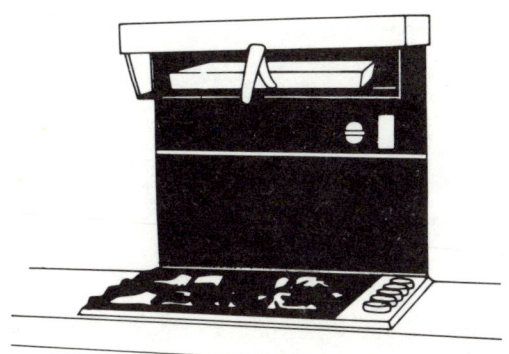

A combined gas hob and grill

A gas-fired built-in hob

temperatures; others prefer electricity which maintains an even temperature and can offer other features.

But, whichever type of cooker—and usually replanning coincides with a possible replacement—consider what it is that you want from your cooker.

List all the factors that are important for you in the cooker.

1. Do you want a free-standing all-in-one cooker, either gas or electric? A single unit or a range?
2. Is the cooker easy to move out of its space for cleaning?
3. Is the hob section easy to clean (sometimes gas cookers are more difficult to clean, although like electric cookers they are now available with sealed drip trays round the burners)?
4. Are the rings and discs on the electric cooker easy to remove and replace?
5. Is ignition to all the gas burners automatic, including grill and ovens.
6. Is there a simmering control on the cooker?
7. Is the grill in the right place—eye level, below the hotplate or in the oven—to suit you?
8. Is the oven the right size?
9. Is the oven self-cleaning? Is it easy to clean? Are there non-stick linings?
10. Is the oven automatic? Are there any other special cooking features, say a rôtisserie?
11. Are there two ovens—one for cooking, the other for warming/cooking?
12. Does the oven have a light inside?
13. Is there a glass door, or double doors?

The Europa Circulaire, a luxury built-in **Creda** plan range. It has glass oven doors and a fan-assisted oven as well as other refinements

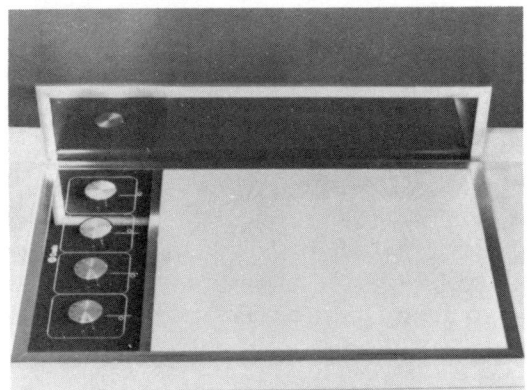

Counter top cooking An inset ceramic hob in a counter top

Gas-fired built-in hob

You may find the answer to your cooker dream is an all-in-one unit with the features you want, or you may find that the cooker to suit your needs is a split-level combination of separate hob and oven. You may decide on an electric oven (some have integral grills and roasting spits) and a gas hob, or vice versa; in some instances you can even have a combination gas/electric hob.

In a split-level situation, the hob will sit anywhere on the counter top (gas and/or electric connections having been calculated, of course); and the oven can be built into a cupboard, making use of a recess in the wall or even an old fireplace, utilising every inch of available working space.

In addition to the electric and gas hot plates there are now ceramic hobs whose flat glazed surfaces are effective in conducting heat to the pans. Even more advanced ceramic hobs using a special heat induction process makes the food and the pans hot, but stay cool to the touch (but, they tend to be rather expensive).

Free-standing cookers, too, now have ceramic hot plates.

And, a word about cooking ranges, either oil, solid fuel or perhaps electrically fired (these are usually found in country areas where gas is not connected); these are expensive to buy but do repay with instant heat for cooking and buckets of hot water, while providing extra warmth in the house during the winter.

Refrigerators

Like cookers, these are available in all sizes and capacities—for fitting under work tops or for building into cupboards or housings or simply as free-standing units.

In most cases they have doors which open within their widths and with optional right- or left-hand openings.

If you are considering buying one, do get the right size—it is better to have a larger refrigerator than a smaller one, constantly regretting the cramped storage available. The rule of thumb here is to allow for a *minimum* of

1 cubic foot capacity per family member *plus* 1 cubic foot to spare.

The things to consider are: Is its size adequate for the family's needs (do not forget families grow)? How efficient is the freezing section and how long can one keep food in the freezer section? Freezer compartments of modern refrigerators are marked with stars, from one to three, to show safe storage time in the freezer, * up to one week, ** up to one month, *** up to three months.

Does the refrigerator defrost automatically? Can it be moved out easily for cleaning?

In some instances it is worth investing in a combined refrigerator/freezer which can be built into the kitchen unit arrangement. Remember that built-in units need ventilation to take away generated heat.

One of **Miele's** combined refrigerators and freezer units, there are, of course, others available

Freezers

Freezers are worth their salt for a large family or for a working family which has minimal time to spare for preparing and cooking food.

There are two types—the upright (vertical) freezer from the small-sized table top model—which can sit comfortably on the top of a refrigerator—to a very large capacity sophisticated 'cupboard'; and the chest freezer which is top or 'lid' opening.

Upright freezers are easier to use. You can see what is in them more easily—for stocking and for rotating the food stored in them; but they are more costly to run because they tend to lose cold air when the door is opened up for use.

The chest freezer is usually less expensive to buy and run, is usually quite large but is more difficult to use. You have to bend over to sort out the food, load or unload it. And you are forever shifting baskets and moving food up from the bottom which can be awkward and heavy work.

Generally, unless you have a really large kitchen, freezers are cumbersome and space wasting, so they are best kept in a cooler place, like a garage or perhaps a cupboard under the stairs but relatively near the kitchen.

Freezers suitable for the kitchen are the smaller table-top variety or the medium-sized vertical models which can be built into a housing, twinning, perhaps, with an in-built refrigerator.

It is a matter of budget and space gain, but your kitchen, if not ideal at the time of planning, should allow for the possibility of including this unit eventually.

Dishwashers

If you have a large family or entertain a lot then a dishwasher as part of your kitchen will become your best friend. This additional pair of hands will cope with that tedious chore, washing-up, efficiently and very hygienically, as it gets rid of bacteria that the most fastidious handwashing and drying cannot do. (It is also an extra working crockery cupboard for you.)

If you decide to get one, consider its capacity. You should be able to load at least two-meal loads of china and cutlery—some can even take pots and pans.

Running the machine when not fully loaded means you are throwing good money away on an expensive toy. Remember all equipment must work for you.

Check the size, capacity, running costs and noise! If it is too noisy it can drive you out of the kitchen.

If you get one, site it near the sink, preferably under the worktop so that there is a suitable plumbing point.

Laundry equipment Making the most of limited space in the kitchen is this stackable pair of units—the Creda Super De Luxe washing machine (front loading) and the Creda Sensamatic tumble dryer

Laundry equipment

If you have to use the kitchen as a laundry, then you will have allowed for its separate activity zone in your plan.

Whatever type of washing machine you have, automatic or twin tub, there must be a water supply and waste outlet next to it as well as a safe electrical connection.

Less space is taken up in the kitchen by front loading machines and hot air tumble dryers, as they can stack, one above the other; but do remember that as there must be adequate ventilation when drying clothes, the machine should either be vented to an outside wall or be placed near a window or strong extractor.

The foremost advantage of having laundry equipment in the kitchen is that it can be supervised easily while the housewife gets on with her 'chores'.

Of course, it is not the best of places to keep the machine, but if it is necessary to launder in the kitchen area through lack of space elsewhere, then utilise the machine's top for an extra working top (protected, of course, to prevent scratching), or alternatively, as an extra meal-top space.

Obviously it is necessary to ensure that the washing machine is suitably positioned as far as plumbing and the water waste pipes are concerned, so that minimal expense is incurred when the washing machine is plumbed in.

It is not a good idea to put the tumble dryer in the kitchen area, unless the kitchen is very large, as warm, moist air can be a nuisance as well as unhealthy; and there is the noise factor, too. Both washing machines and tumble dryers are noisy, and this can be more than a bearable nuisance.

Light, air and warmth

Light, Air and Warmth

Comfort while working in the kitchen is not only determined by the working heights of units and the efficiency of equipment, but also by the right levels and balance of heat, ventilation and light.

Background heating

Although most kitchens generate a certain amount of heat of their own once general activity gets under way, a certain degree of background heating is needed so that the room is comfortable to work in, particularly first thing on a frosty winter's morning.

Check your plan to see that you have made allowances for this. For those kitchens with limited floor space, a wall-hung electric convector heater will suffice. Alternatively a radiant infra-red heater can be used, although this only heats a limited area.

There is also bound to be enough room to take a free-standing portable oil-filled electric radiator or fan heater.

Should you have a central heating system, the answer could be a length of skirting heating in place of a conventional radiator.

If your kitchen has a brick, stone or quarry tiled floor then electric under-floor heating could be put in but it is a major job and tends to be expensive to run.

Ventilation

Apart from heat for comfort, it is essential to have good ventilation in any kitchen. A steamy atmosphere and the minute particles of grease-laden dust automatically found in the kitchen will spoil its decor and general appearance (to say nothing of the lingering smell of yesterday's supper!) Walls, ceilings and cupboards become discoloured and paintwork soon suffers, and in some cases mould appears.

To overcome the problem take stock of the situation:

- Avoid condensation on windows, at least in part by using double glazing—and there are many systems available from sophisticated

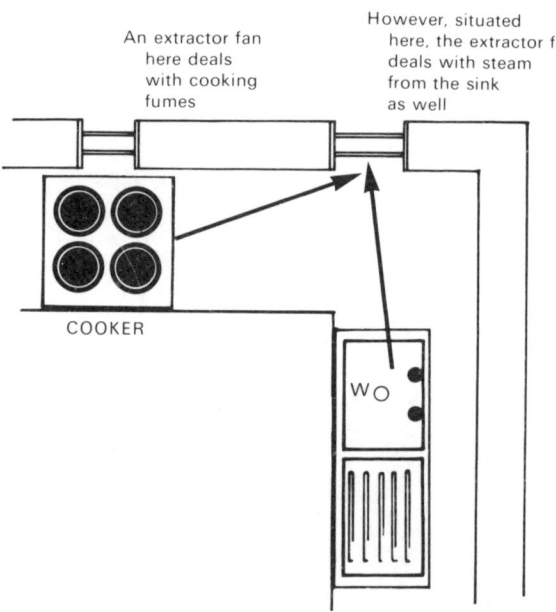

An extractor fan here deals with cooking fumes

However, situated here, the extractor fan deals with steam from the sink as well

COOKER

An extractor fan, strategically positioned, can keep the kitchen sweet-smelling and steam-free

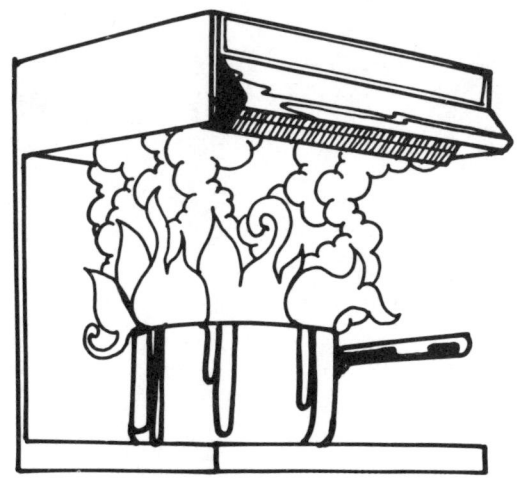

Cooker hoods A re-circulatory cooker hood, using an activated charcoal filter, cleans and re-circulates air into the kitchen

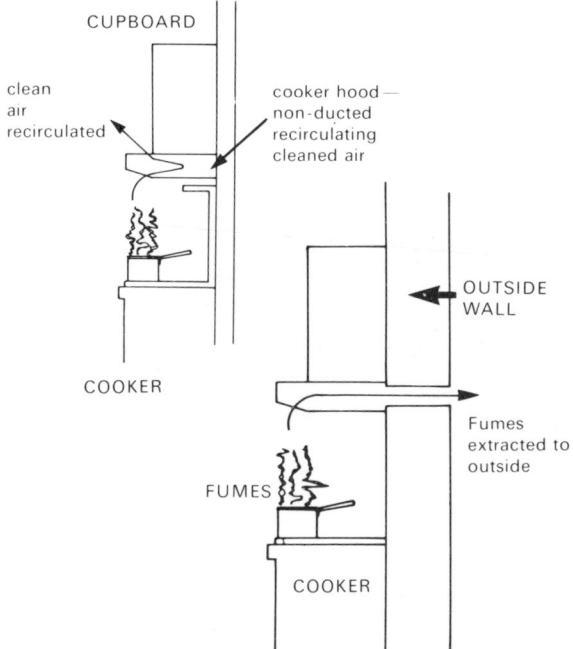

A ducted cooker hood, right, extracts fumes and steam to the outside

- For the small kitchen, an electrically driven window fan can be used to change the air—or an extractor fitted in the wall at a strategic point near the steam's source could do the trick. These should be capable of extracting some 500 cu m (1800 cu ft) per hour of air, and have a shutter when not in use.

- But for large areas, the window or wall extractor is not powerful enough. Cooker hobs (especially gas-fired ones) are the main culprits, usually being positioned well away from windows, and needing to be well ventilated. The answer here is an electrically operated cooker hood with variable speeds. Cooker hoods work in two ways. First there is the ductless type which purifies the air by sucking it through filters (usually charcoal). The cleaned air is then re-circulated. Fine wire mesh or foam plastic filters inside the hood trap the air-borne grease. These are easily changed or washed to make sure they work efficiently. The stronger and more efficient type of cooker hood is ducted to the outside, where the smells, water vapour and grease particles are discharged, as well as some of the excess heat generated by the cooker.

If you do a lot of cooking, the ducted cooker hood is the answer. To work efficiently, the space between the cooker top and the underside of the hood should not be more than 560 mm (22 in) or it will not work efficiently.

Extractor fans in windows, well away from the cooker units—ovens and hobs—tend to spread smells and steam around and thus are ineffective.

sealed units to d.i.y. kits. However, where water vapour is excessive the answer must be to install an extractor fan.

An **Atag** ceramic hob on the working surface with a glass-fronted electric oven underneath. The cooker hood helps to reduce condensation

Lighting

Your kitchen should enjoy the best of both natural daylight and artificial light. It plays such an important part in the kitchen design that its correct use and level of intensity cannot be over-emphasised.

From the smallest to the largest kitchens the lighting should be efficient and stimulating but not over-demanding so that your eyes become strained and tired.

Plan your lighting, slotting it into four distinct areas.

- General diffused overall lighting for the kitchen as a whole.
- Working surface lighting—which should be strong and clear and localised.
- Cupboard lighting / eating area lighting.
- Equipment lighting—as in ovens, refrigerators, cooker hoods, also on some cooker tops.

Ideally your kitchen should have a mixture of these forms of lighting so that each centre of activity is catered for and colour values (which apply to food as well as decor) are maintained.

Natural daylight

First comes natural daylight and the position of your window(s). The more natural light the better. You will find that most local authorities stipulate the window area in the kitchen to be at least one-tenth of the floor area of the room—and one half of this must be openable. So, if you are enlarging an existing window, bear this in mind.

Also consider the following in conjunction with your kitchen plan:
1. A corner window will illuminate all of the adjacent wall, while a centrally positioned window leaves both corners in shadow.
2. A high-positioned window throws light far back into the room, while

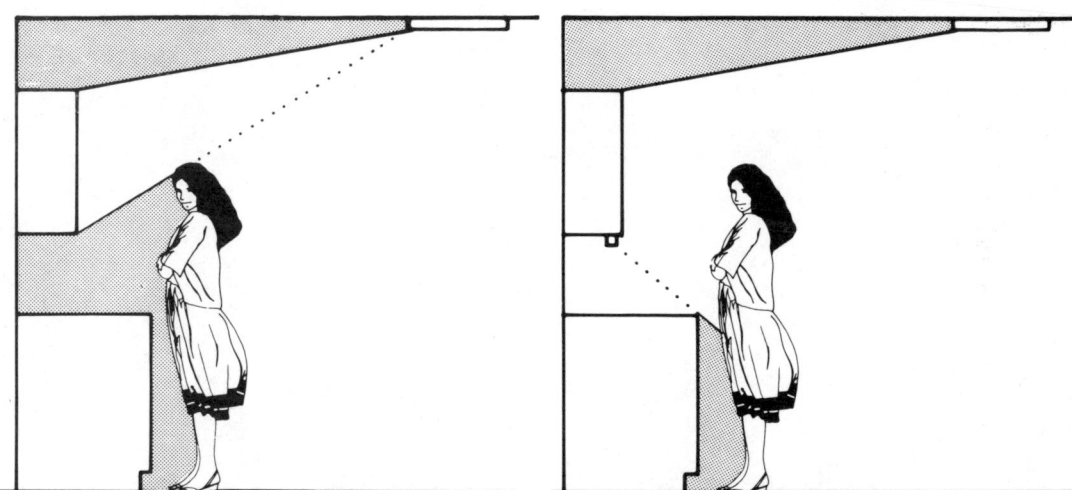

Do not work in your own light, as you can cast shadows on what you are doing. Do put lighting strips under the cupboard fronts (with a protective baffle) to downlight what you are doing

conversely a low-placed window cuts off the light half way down the wall.

3. For the best lighting in a kitchen the window should be east-facing. With west or south facing windows the intensity of light and possibly heat (particularly during the summer) will be overpowering.

4. North facing windows have no direct access to the sun but because the light is clear, provide a pleasant lighting level.

General lighting

Depending upon your kitchen's size and plan you will probably need at least one if not two ceiling fittings strategically positioned to give adequate all-over lighting. Do remember to take into account where the secondary lighting is to be placed for your specific work centres.

Working surface lighting

Working surface lighting and secondary lighting should be concealed strip

Nairn Cushionflor Super Classic Dahlia is used in this **Grovewood** kitchen. Note the pendant light above the dining area, just where direct light should be

lights in 'warm white', preferably with diffusers, set behind a continuous run of wall cupboards or fixed to the underside front edge of wall cupboards. These illuminate the worktop without glare.

Downlighters, too, can be fixed into the bottom of wall cabinets to throw down pools of light onto the worktop below.

Another means of localised lighting is to use adjustable ceiling hung spot lights, so that they can be directed onto wall cupboards or working areas.

A light directed downwards onto the eating area is ideal where you eat in larger kitchens. A rise-and-fall pendant light would perhaps also suit here, depending on the room's décor.

Cupboard and equipment lighting

These are self-explanatory, but one must stress, necessary, to prevent eye strain and accidents.

Dimmer switches are invaluable for altering the intensity levels of the lighting, and can produce dramatic changes to the kitchen's general appearance.

Do remember

1. You must never stand in your own shadow while you are working, so make sure the light is ahead of you or to the side but never behind.
2. Avoid a uniform high level of illumination as this is particularly harsh and tiring.
3. Allow more light in a room which is dark or has dark furniture or decor.
4. Try to avoid high-gloss surfaces— like shiny worktops, shiny tiles and glossy floors. These are all reflective. If you cannot avoid their use adjust the lighting levels as much as possible.
5. Never use tungsten strip lights under cupboards as they get too hot for safety.
6. Lowering a ceiling means you can inset lights.
7. An all-over illuminated ceiling is the answer for some to glare-free working. Translucent plastic or acrylic sheet forms the suspended ceiling behind which the light fittings, usually fluorescent strips, are fixed.
8. Should your kitchen have two entrances, you will need a two-way switching system to prevent groping along the kitchen wall for a single light switch.

The finishing touches

Producing a pleasantly styled kitchen is like making a cake—its success depends upon how skilful you are in selecting and mixing your ingredients. Look at what you have—an improved or new layout—with all equipment sited accordingly.

Now it is time to marry up the practical aspects of the design with aesthetic appeal, for the colour scheme and materials chosen are very important and can make or mar the finished kitchen.

Colour

Attitudes towards colour in the home have changed dramatically over recent years; now there is an alert colour awareness and never more so than for kitchens. There is no longer a typical kitchen colour scheme; instead an across-the-board choice from white and pastels to bold colours as well as natural 'back to nature' tones (found in slate, wood, brick, cork). Helping to achieve this are paints, wallcoverings, kitchen units, working surfaces, even cooker fronts and refrigerators, as well as pots and pans. Changes can be achieved from the serene to the exotic and you do not need a bottomless purse for this.

Accepting the fact that kitchen colour schemes are subject to fashion, like the clothes we wear, they should be trendy to a degree but also comfortable.

Now, think carefully—could you live with a colour combination for say, ten years? This is thought to be the lifespan for kitchen equipment and flooring, and in some ways, for walls, too.

There is no point in being daring if you are going to get tired of your surroundings after perhaps two years, as it is a costly exercise. On the other hand if you plan to use things which are relatively inexpensive to achieve an imaginative effect—like paint or wallpaper on the walls and vinyl on the floor rather than ceramic tiles or wood panelling for walls and ceramic tiles on the floor—then you can ring the changes at a reasonable cost.

Work out a set of rules for colour scheming. Some of us possess less natural colour sense than others, so general hints and guidelines on what colours or tones to choose are useful.

According to expert colour consultants different colours produce definite moods:

1. Saffron or sunflower yellow is warm and cheerful, so are orange and coral.
2. Bright red is stimulating and cheerful.
3. Some forms of mid-blue, like cornflower or hyacinth, are also cheerful. If dark blue or blue with a greenish tinge is used, this can be cold and depressing.
4. Shades of green, from lettuce to lime, are pleasant, fresh and for some, calming.

5. Dark reds, purple and navy can be dramatic or depressing, so need teaming with light accessories for a lift.
6. Black, dark brown can also be overpowering and dramatic so team them with vibrant and neutral accents.
7. White is a neutral, usually aesthetically pleasing, but if used without some contrast, can be cold and clinical.
8. Neutral colours, beiges, light and mid-brown and some forms of grey, found in natural materials are generally acceptable on their own, but are better when used to enhance a colour scheme.

Remember the aspect of your room makes a difference to the chosen colour scheme. North facing light is cold and clear yet can be hard; use a warm toned scheme to balance it, while a south facing aspect means using cooler colours.

In the end, colour theory when applied is only a means of confirming or modifying your personal selection.

With a colour scheme in mind you can now look at the largest areas in the kitchen, the floor and walls: both have a considerable bearing on the scheme as a whole.

Floor

The floor presents an even, flat effect in contrast to the walls so colour and design are important here.

If you decide you need a new floor-covering it should be durable, easy to clean, comfortable to walk on, safe (non-slippery) and have a minimum of seams and joins which must be well secured.

Kentish Tile, a traditional quarry tile effect in **Marley** Vinylaire Spring range – ideal for kitchen floors as it is resilient and good looking

Your choice is overwhelming in the two main flooring categories—hard floors and resilient floors.

Hard floors
These include quarry tiles, stone flags, terrazzo, bricks and ceramic tiles; also wood blocks and planking. All are extremely hard-wearing, relatively easy to keep clean and when put down are virtually indestructible. However, apart from the wood, they are not so comfortable to walk on, are not resilient and tend to be cold and noisy underfoot—in addition they are not kind to crocks and dishes if accidentally dropped on them.

Resilient floors
These comprise cork (sheet or tile) supplied sealed or unsealed. Cork is very comfortable to walk on and warm to touch, with fine insulating values both for heat and acoustics.

Linoleum (also sheet and tiles) now not in plentiful supply, is extremely hardwearing if correctly put down and looked after.

Vinyl sheet and tiles are offered in a huge design and colour choice. Some tiles are made with an adhesive backing for the proficient handyman to put down.

Cushioned vinyl (pvc sheeting which is usually latex backed, or sometimes felt or foam backed) now leads in popularity for kitchen floorcoverings. There are several grades, geared to different budgets and an almost limitless number of patterns and colourways. The emphasis is now on hygenic 'seamless' floors, which like tufted carpets come extra wide and so avoid joins—a boon for safety (no tripping on seams) and hygiene (no dirt traps at the joins).

Carpet is also made for kitchens. Synthetic fibres are used here in fine, looped pile on springy latex backing. The surface is treated sometimes to shrug off dirt and stains and is easy to clean.

Carpet tiles, too, are now being used in kitchens and offer a number of advantages. Individual tiles can be replaced if damaged; stains can be washed off under a tap, and tiles can be moved around to even out wear.

Another resilient floor with good insulating properties is flooring grade chipboard. When stained or varnished it looks attractive yet is practical and gives a stable, even floor.

All resilient floorings wear well if chosen carefully and put down properly. Make sure all floors are level and damp proof before you cover them. In older houses a self-levelling screed or hardboard or chipboard, or even marine plywood should be used as a level underfloor before the final surface is put down.

Two plus factors for resilient floors are comfort under foot and less liklihood of breakages if things are dropped on them.

Textured surfaces are usually non-slip and, from a practical point of view, tend not to show minor blemishes and marks, including general wear and tear.

If the kitchen door leads directly to the garden, it is worth using a mat well at the threshold to trap the dirt and grit before this is trodden into the kitchen floor damaging it. Insetting the mat means it does not stand proud, so you cannot trip over it.

Wall finishes

What you use to decorate your kitchen walls merits an important place in your scheme. Here contrasts are provided between the hard and soft, rough and smooth, also in reflecting and non-reflecting surfaces, as light strikes them at different angles, producing these effects.

Whatever you choose, they should be easy to clean.

Ceramic tiles are generally the most practical for behind the worktop, round the cooker and as a sink splashback, as they resist water and heat and wipe clean very easily. If you tile throughout you will not need to decorate for years to come, but to do so can be expensive.

If possible try to use tiles with matt or semi-matt surfaces rather than high gloss, as these cut down glare and condensation.

Wood (panels or tongued and grooved boards) is an ideal wall-covering, provided of course the battens to which it is fixed is treated with preservative against possible damp. It is an ideal insulant as air is trapped between the walls and the wood.

Cork tiles or panels, too, preferably sealed, give added warmth and are practical. Smooth or textured surfaces are available as well as different sizes.

Stainless steel tiles also look good as well as being practical. Apart from the silver finish, old gold, bronze and copper shades are available.

Paint, ubiquitous and practical, offers the largest choice in type and colour. For kitchens, emulsion or eggshell finishes, rather than gloss, are best as they are non-reflective and tend to mask any condensation.

Colour choice is unlimited, if you cannot find a standard shade, it can be custom-mixed for you. Also, paint is an excellent cosmetic, hiding a multitude of sins.

Coated, plasticised or vinyl wallpapers are easy to use. Their big plus is that when you tire of them they can be changed and replaced easily, like paint. Hundreds of designs and colours exist to suit any taste.

If you decide on a bold pattern, however, do remember that your everyday things in the kitchen from clocks to pots also provide pattern and colour, so should be integrated as well.

Plastic laminate, colourful, practical and hygienic is also suitable for wallcovering round the work centres, provided joins and edges are properly sealed. Do not use it round the cooker area as plastic laminate is affected by direct heat and can scorch and burn.

Brickwork, too, is the ultimate for some people as wall surfaces. Being a natural material, most things in a colour scheme blend or harmonise with it, not only in tone but in textural feel.

If you have had to do considerable renovations prior to re-planning, why not leave the brickwork exposed as a decor feature?

Units/cupboards

Colour chosen for cupboard or unit fronts plays a major role in the integrated kitchen.

New units today offer a wide choice of colour, texture and finish, so there is bound to be something to suit everyone.

The most popular surface treatments are sheet plastic laminate veneers or melamine coats, offering plain colours, wood grains, simulated hessian and linen, even suede finishes — depending upon your budget.

The trend towards 'things natural and homely' is reflected across the complete decor scene from floorcoverings to units, so one sees an increasing number of kitchen units made in wood or with wood effect finishes, sporting slatted doors or fielded panels, contributing to this rustic feeling. There are also units with real rattan cane, linen and fabric fronts in keeping with this theme.

The rustic trend is not confined to expensive ranges, but is available in 'knock down' kit kitchen ranges from a variety of sources—cash and carry discount companies with national distribution d.i.y. outlets, mail order companies, departmental stores and so on. These, with readily available whitewood (unfinished) furniture which one can paint, veneer or varnish, allows the proficient handyman to achieve his ideal at down to earth cost.

Working surfaces

These surfaces should complement the surrounding units, floor and walls.

Generally plastic laminates are used, which choice offers plain colours, marble, wood grains, linen, cork, hessian, ginghams, hewn stone—virtually any effect, matt or glossy finished.

Remember that plastic does scratch and mark if mis-used, so do not chop or cut on it. Instead, set in a wooden chopping board.

Pieces of slate or marble have cool surfaces and are ideal for rolling out pastry, so consider setting one of these in the worktop. And for a pan rest, why not a section of stainless steel next to the cooker? It is practical and indestructible.

Making headway as a working surface is ceramic tiling. No worries here about chopping, cutting, or resting hot pans, but take care with china or you may damage both the crocks and the tile surface.

Window treatments

These are an integral part of the kitchen. The object is not to impede natural daylight, but a touch of colour can enhance a window's appeal. Rather than curtains (if used, they should be non-flammable, like glass fibre), give the area a roller blind treatement—preferable to venetian blinds which accumulate greasy kitchen dust and are difficult to clean.

If the commercially available roller blinds do not suit your decor, there are easy to assemble kits available, where you use your own material.

For textured surfaces you could use bamboo or even pinoleum (slivers of pine wood) roller blinds.

Aide memoire and cosmetic treatments

Now it is rethink time on your plan. Be it minor alterations or a massive change of layout the same advice applies—make sure you have what you want exactly where you want it; nothing should be left to chance.

You are probably quite capable of doing some tasks, others will need expert attention if you are unsure about them. But whether you or an expert does the job, the work involved must be co-ordinated to save time, expense and aggravation.

1. Look at the kitchen—walls, floor and ceilings—to check for rising damp, wet and dry rot, bad drainage. Existing gas or water pipes may have to be sealed off, diverted, extended or even replaced. Outside drains may need attention.

   If major work has to be done to put things right wait until this is done before actually drawing-up your final layout; after all, repairs may affect the size and shape of the room and thus have a bearing on the plan.

2. Now consider the electrics. In old houses it is better to put in a new ring circuit rather than overload an existing out-of-date system. At the same time, make sure your future needs will be met with extra switched double socket outlets.

3. Next focus on the sink plumbing and decide on what sort of hot water supply is necessary. Heating hot water for the whole house might be from a hot-water storage cylinder— part of a central heating system—or an immersion heated tank. In old houses storage tanks are usually located a long way from the kitchen so water has to travel via long pipe runs which are expensive to install and heat-wasting.

   Your answer could be a 'point of use' water heater fixed over or under the sink (this must be on an outside wall) and connected to the cold water supply—either gas or electrically heated.

4. At this point, too, fit stopcocks for hot and cold water pipes; permanently fix the sink, connecting the supply; wire up the lights, switches and socket outlets.

5. If you already have a telephone in the house, it makes sense to have a wall telephone extension fixed in the kitchen. Do this before decorating or cupboard fixing.

6. Decide on your wall surfaces. If they are to be tiled, should this be before or after fitting your cupboards? When a cupboard butts against a return wall, the wall should be tiled *first,* so it does not interfere with the opening of a door or drawer.

   When tiles are only going to be used between the working surface and the underside of the units, then fix them *after* the units are put up. Always make allowances for the thickness of wall and floor tiles when you are planning. That extra millimetre or two can make a difference!

7. If you are wood cladding or panelling walls, the same thing applies, only you must make allowances when you are battening to provide additional battens at strategic lines around the room to coincide exactly with the screw fixings for the cupboards. Also allow extra battens where you know shelves, spice racks and kitchen tool holders will be fixed. Do not forget a possible cooker hood.

8. Decorating and other finishing touches are completed at the end of the plan of campaign. These can include putting down floorcovering or renovating existing floors, painting and wall finishing.

Cosmetic Treatments

Where it is a case of a tight budget preventing—for the time being—any major buys, it should not stop you from trying to make the best of what you have. With a number of suggestions and ideas for existing cupboards and surfaces as well as a few inexpensive additions, you can make a silk purse out of a sow's ear.

Kitchen cupboards and shelves

Having taken stock of the new layout it is a matter of deciding whether or not you use the existing kitchen cupboards or invest in new ones. Take a long look at your things; if they are basically sound, roomy but not necessarily modern, do not replace them yet, but give them a face-lift. You will be surprised at what a little patience can do.

1. First, why not just change the colour? This is one of the easiest solutions. Stripping off old paint and making good the surface, priming and then repainting to suit the whole new colour scheme you have chosen.
It can be an all-over colour or doors and drawers can contrast with the rest of the cupboard.

2. An alternative is to strip back to bare wood with a liquid paint stripper and, after sanding smooth, apply a wood varnish. If it is a light pine or ash effect you want, simply use a clear polyurethane varnish (matt or lustre). If you want a distinctive colour like teak, mahogany, oak or even a bright pop colour (red, green or yellow) then use a combined stain/varnish. The finished effect is very attractive.

3. High gloss painted or spray finished doors that are even and flat, could have a plastic laminate finish in one of the hundreds of designs/colourways available.

4. Why not cover the cupboard fronts with an adhesive-backed vinyl fabric? These are readily available and come in a huge variety of finishes and designs. Either cover the units all over or use the fabric for contrast with a painted background. The permutations are endless.

5. On the same theme, once the door and drawer fronts have been resurfaced, why not emphasise their edges with mouldings.

6. Use a vinyl wallpaper, to match one you are using, on the cupboard fronts. Alternatively, paste on plasticised material to match your new roller blinds. You can then use a

moulding round the edge of the door, leave it plain, or cut out a thin plywood shaped facing to fit over the top. This can be painted to match-in with the rest of the kitchen's scheme.

7. Use fretted hardboard on the cupboard fronts with the painted surfaces showing through like a stencil.
8. Surprisingly, just using a wallpaper border or strip of pattern from the wallpaper being used to fix round the edge of a cupboard front or drawer is effective.
9. Invest in some attractive door handles or pulls to replace existing ones. If you now have a farm-style scheme, use brass handles or knobs. Alternatively, use aluminium moulding with in-built finger pulls to give a streamlined look to the cupboards instead of conventional handles.
10. If the cupboards are sound but old fashioned why not replace the doors? You can buy panelled or louvre doors in various sizes at much less than buying a completely new cupboard.
11. Two floor-standing cupboards joined together and unified by a single working top makes an ideal peninsular unit.

    If the back of each unit is removed and doors fitted, the things stored inside are accessible from both sides. This is particularly useful if sets of drawers and wire baskets are used inside to replace shelves. They can be withdrawn and pushed back from either side.
12. With a view to a double lease of life, why not use a chest of drawers as a store cupboard—provided you reinforce the bottom of each drawer. Old furniture or whitewood units are ideal for this. After serving its purpose, the chest can revert back to its traditional use.

Shelves

For some, new cupboards are out of the question or may be non-existent, but there is no reason why shelves cannot be used instead.

1. If you have old ones, give them a beauty treatment—surface over with wipe-clean plastic laminate veneer, including the front edge.
2. Alternatively, ceramic tile over, using round edged tiles along the front to prevent a sharp edge.
3. Make shelves from ready laminated lengths of board, cut to fit.

Roller blinds

Roller blinds are useful for a number of purposes apart from prettying up windows.

1. Hide unsightly but necessary shelves behind ceiling-hung roller blinds; when unrolled they are pleasant to look at but obscure the view.

    Match the blinds to the window for a co-ordinated look.
2. Roller blinds are useful for hiding things like alcoves, as substitutes for doors, as room dividers, particularly if you eat in the kitchen—the working section is at least temporarily hidden.

Sinks

It is unhygienic to keep a cracked china or chipped enamel sink. Replace it with a new one. This might be your one major buy at the outset but it is worth it for hygiene as well as being a practical purchase. It is an investment, too.

If the sink is not too bad, but the taps are worn, then a quick change is made by using a tap-top conversion kit (most builders and plumbers merchants, and d.i.y. outlets have them).

Working surfaces

You might not be able to fit a run of floor cupboards, but you can, temporarily, unify an area by putting on a length of worktop.

1. Use ready laminated lengths of working top; these come in various lengths and thicknesses. Fix at a convenient height and secure well. The space underneath is extra storage.
2. A badly marked plastic laminated worktop can be revitalised. If possible prise off the old laminate and put on a new veneer. (Re-laminating directly on top of the old is not usually successful as the under laminate may be unstable and lift, taking the new veneer with it.)
3. You can use ceramic tiles, and as with the shelves, remember to use round-edged tiles along the front edge to prevent cut fingers.

Extra table/counter

Where there is little room for an upright table you can fix a table top directly to the wall to flap down when not in use. Make sure it is supported by wall fixed pivoting arms when it is being used.

Or, under an existing length of worktop, why not fix another counter section which can be extended to make an eating counter or more working surface—this is a boon in narrow kitchens.

Spaces to spare

Where you have spaces between floor cupboards and you want to hide them (particularly if it is where you keep the vegetables, for instance), then use fretted hardboard, on frames, doubling as decorative doors which are easily painted and ideal for allowing free ventilation.

Ceilings

There are a number of things one can do to improve ceilings.

1. If it is very high, paint it a dark colour to make it appear lower (this can also hide ugly pipework).
2. If it is in a tatty, cracked condition, after making good, use a textured paint for a permanent rough-cast finish.
3. Give a lofty ceiling a new dimension by lowering it; suspend a false ceiling, say tongued and grooved boards or panels—this can be stunning.
4. Introduce wooden beams across the ceiling at a comfortable low level to introduce a country feeling to the room—especially if the beams are dark and the ceiling white; conversely if the beams are white and the ceiling dark. You also have good possibilities to be imaginative here with lighting (concealed or otherwise).

Lights

New light fittings need not be expensive. National chain stores sell a wide variety of fittings from tungsten fluorescent tubes to pendant lamps and spot lights.

Refrigerators

An old refrigerator can have a new lease of life with a covering of adhesive-backed vinyl fabric.

But you can do great things with paint, provided you rub down the old paint surfaces ready to key for the new coat.

You may even be able to persuade a local car spraying outfit to give the refrigerator a new paint coat, and in any colour you choose (cars come in all colours these days!).

Floors

Flooring grade chipboard when poly-urethaned makes an attractive floor, as mentioned previously. At a later stage it serves as a sub-floor for ceramic tiles, vinyl tiles, vinyl sheet or carpet.

Old quarry tiles, stone flags or even bricks can be revitalised by using a scarfing machine (you hire these) to remove grime, surface grind and seal. There are chemical treatments available to remove stubborn stains, and there are also dyes for brick to give it a new lease of life.

Wooden floors, too, can be refurbished by using a sanding machine, then varnishing or painting over.

Walls

Be a little imaginative and turn what could be a disaster area into something attractive, including that ugly fireplace.

The main culprits are disintegrating plastered walls, crying out for replacement.

1. Remove the old plaster and expose the brickwork as a feature. Well wire brushed and cleaned (discoloura-tions are removed by special chemical treatments) then sealed with transparent waterproofing solu-tion, the natural brick walls are an attractive asset. If you prefer the texture but not the colour, emulsion paint the bricks. Think of the money saved in not replastering!

Doorways

One or two things can be done here:
1. Glazing a door in the kitchen adds more light.
2. Making a stable door—one which is in two independent halves, hori-zontally—is interesting and helpful if you want to keep an eye on the children next door but deny them access to the kitchen.
3. If you do not want a conventional door, use a folding fabric door, a sliding door, or ranch-style cowboy swing doors—easily obtained at d.i.y. outlets.

Inexpensive kitchen ranges

Bearing in mind how expensive some kitchen units are, it is worth con-sidering investing in some whitewood units, or in the kit-type kitchens you assemble yourself and sometimes finish off, as well.

There are two ways of looking at this type of investment. By investing a few pounds in materials for perking up the kitchen generally you can count on saving treble your outlay at least if you were to buy new units.

But, by investing in medium-priced units which you are able to finish off yourself, you may have sufficient money over for one or two luxuries otherwise denied you.

Safety in the kitchen

Because of the many potential dangers lurking in the kitchen, especially for young children and the elderly, take care to avoid every possible hazard.

A disturbing fact is that as many accidents occur in the home as on the roads due to the various activities going on in the busiest room in the house. Take a long, hard look at your kitchen plan and within it try to take sensible precautions.

Children

If youngsters have to play in the kitchen, try to keep the play area well away from the cooking centre if possible. Persuade them to be tidy at least and not leave their toys scattered around . . . it only needs a step on a small toy to turn an ankle or even break a leg!

Use a pan guard to prevent children from trying to touch handles on the cooker, or, at least turn the saucepan handles and spouts away from the cooker front.

Never carry hot foods, kettles or saucepans when young children are around your feet, and never pass hot things over their heads.

Never keep matches at fingertip level, little ones are notoriously curious and like playing with new 'toys'.

Also never leave electric sockets 'naked' at ground level (if sockets have to be here) at least cover these with 'blind' plugs when not in use.

Control knobs on any appliance should be well out of a child's reach.

If there is any way of making a kitchen child-proof and safe, do so. Use, say, an extending gate to prevent crawling infants and toddlers from wandering about, or if it is possible, consider a stable door as mentioned in Chapter 9.

Floors

Try to avoid smooth, slippery flooring — ceramics and some vinyls are notoriously slippery when they are wet; mop up and dry these surfaces as soon as possible after washing down or after spills.

If you must polish a smooth floor, then at least use a non-slip water based emulsion polish, never a wax polish.

Keep the floor clear of all obstructions, from toys to shopping bags — do not put them down for just a minute — even a brush and pan.

Do not use mats, but if you have to, then make sure they have a non-slip backing.

Always secure loose edges to linoleum, vinyl, carpeting or floor tiles. Turned-up edges are as much an invitation to trip over as are broken or cracked surfaces.

Stores out of reach

Do not take short cuts when trying to reach high shelves; use a stepladder or a step stool, never a chair. Do not carry too much at one go, you can overbalance—instead, take two journeys.

General stores

As mentioned previously, the most used items of food and equipment should be well within reach.

Keep cupboard doors and drawers closed when not in use. This applies to everything from foodstuffs to household cleaning items. Anything that is potentially dangerous—like polishes, bleach, spirits, silver cleaner—should be stored outside the kitchen. First, because it is safer, and second, because these items are strong smelling and can impregnate other things in nearby cupboards.

If there are youngsters around who are able to touch and experiment with them, the results could spell disaster.

Lighting

All working surfaces must be well lit to prevent accidents and eye strain, there is no excuse saying, 'I couldn't actually see what I was doing'. Do not work in your own shadow.

Power supply

Because electricity is not tangible, visible or audible, except when in use people tend to forget it is there, but this lethal form of energy should be treated with the greatest respect.

Each kitchen should have a minimum of five switched double socket outlets, preferably more, with a number fixed at around 10 mm (4 in) above the worktop level for small appliances. Ideally there should be a socket outlet at each end of a working surface. Fixing them just above the counter means there is no danger of wet cleaning cloths coming into contact with them and causing an accident.

Do not overload outlets with too many appliances or adaptors—this is unnecessary if you have a sufficient number of sockets—as you will overload the circuit and could cause a fire.

Sufficient sockets prevent the dangerous practice of trailing flexes along counter tops or along the floor to an outlet.

Never drape flexes round the taps or anywhere near water. If you have an electric kettle, make sure the socket outlet is quite a way from the sink and water, so that should the lead stray, by chance, it cannot become a lethal weapon.

If appliances do not work, unplug them. Never try to investigate the fault while they are still 'live'. Replace frayed or torn flexes, also broken sockets and plugs.

Make sure your plugs have the correct weight of fuse for the appliance, and unplug them when not in use.

If you suspect an appliance is faulty, do not be neglectful, take it to be repaired or serviced as soon as possible.

When buying electrical appliances look for the electrical industry's mark of approval; this is denoted by the letters BEAB—British Electrotechnical Approvals Board.

Gas appliances

Gas appliances like their electrical counterparts are also tested before being given approval for use by British Gas.

If you think your cooker is faulty, do not delay, contact your local gas industry service department.

Should you smell gas, never try to find the leak yourself, particularly not with a naked flame. Stop people from smoking in the house until the fault has been found. Call your emergency service number—gas, like electricity, is lethal.

Fires

Carelessness is the root cause of most accidents in the kitchen, one of the worst hazards being fire.

Chip pans are notorious for igniting, so too are frying pans. Never fill them more than half full and do not ever leave them unattended or let them overheat.

Do not tip wet food into hot fat; drain it and so prevent spatter. Should the pans catch fire, smother the flames with a damp cloth or a large pan lid. Never move the flaming pan or try to throw it out of a window or door—the draught will bring the flames and contents back and so burn you.

Do not use a toaster near curtains or under cupboard units.

Any material used for kitchen curtains or roller blinds should be non-flammable, like glass fibre.

Do not keep polishes or polishing cloths in confined spaces like under the sink, as the heat can vaporise the chemicals and cause spontaneous combustion.

Do not keep aerosol cans near the cooker or in direct sunlight. They can explode, like bombs.

Do not dry clothes in front of an oven door or on a plate rack over the cooker hob.

If an electrical appliance catches fire, try to unplug it; if this is not possible, then switch off the mains first, then unplug. Never try to put out an electrical fire with water.

If there is a fire of any kind, *do not panic*; see that everyone is out of the room (preferably out of the house), close all doors and call the fire service.

Hygiene

Do not smoke, make-up or do your hair in the kitchen, or groom pets.

Keep pets away from food. Pet food is a possible source of contamination, especially if it is fresh pet meat, so prepare it with a separate set of cutlery and dishes kept for this purpose. Wash all implements and dishes in hot water afterwards, and store well away from crockery and cutlery in general use.

Always wash your hands after fondling pets and before preparing food of any kind.

Never leave food exposed to the atmosphere but cover it over; the same applies in the refrigerator or larder—to prevent possible airborne contamination by germs and insects.

Sterilising worktops

Swab down your plastic laminate working surfaces or ceramic tile tops with a solution of sterilising fluid (not bleach), the type of liquid used to sterilise babies' feeding bottles.

Use the same solution to cleanse plastic washing up bowls, nylon brushes, plastic spoons, non-metallic and nylon pot scourers and dish cloths.

Larder shelves, drawer interiors and

other surfaces should receive this treatment, as should refrigerator interiors.

Remember to wash down the milk bottles or cartons before putting them away in the larder or refrigerator—after all they have been exposed to dirt and germs and handled considerably before reaching you; the same applies to yoghurt cartons.

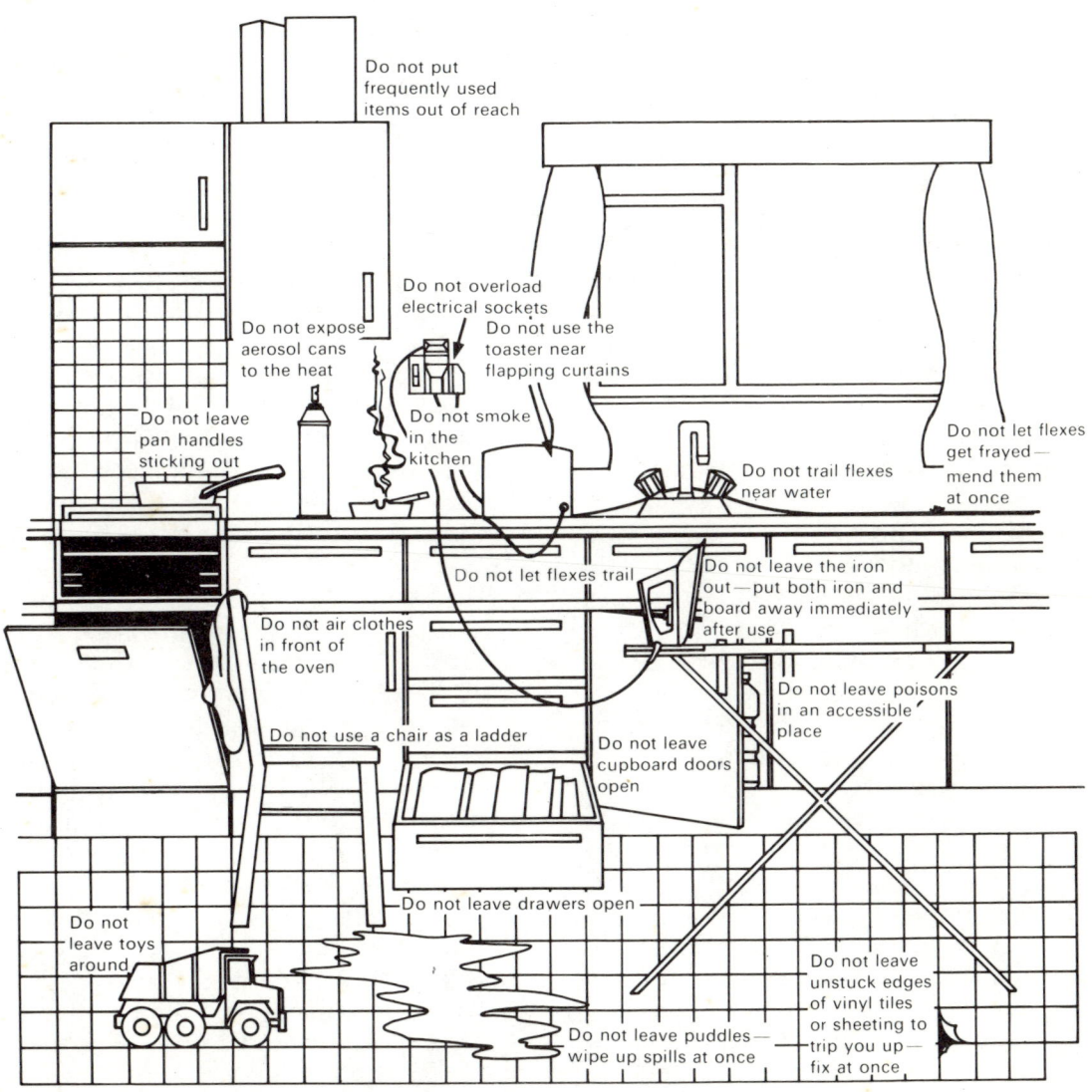

Hazards in a typical kitchen (courtesy of Hygena)

Helping hands

It is one thing having planned or decided on just what you are going to do and quite another actually carrying out the scheme, particularly when it comes to tackling the intricacies of plumbing, electrics, plastering, carpentry and all the other hundred and one things which are essential to bring the design together as a whole.

Those who are lucky enough to be able to hand over the painful business to a builder will not have the worry of actually doing the job but should be sufficiently in the know and have confidence in the people who are.

For many, because of the money involved in doing the job from start to finish, it has to be a proficient handyman effort, with everybody chipping in to do the chores, from demolishing the larder to handing out the nails when the floor is being hardboarded or chipboarded over!

Others, and this usually applies to the majority of us, will tackle just so much on the practical side, but will call in the 'professionals' to do the tricky bits like the re-wiring, plumbing and so on.

However, whichever section you identify with, you should at least be aware of the organisations and associations which can give you advice should you meet a problem.

In some instances, it is a matter of finding out who is a reliable electrician or plumber or central heating engineer.

On the other hand, you may want to compare products like sinks, floorings, ceramic tiles and so on—where can you go to see them or who can you approach to send literature?

Some useful organisations

As a matter of fact there are a considerable number of agencies—from large companies to official bodies, including Government departments—who are willing to help the public, although this is not generally known, so included here in 'Helping Hands' is a list of names and addresses and telephone numbers of those who will help, providing literature on their products, names of stockists in various areas, addresses of local showrooms and so on.

To find professional assistance (and this is not simply consulting the Yellow Pages telephone directory) a list is given of organisations which insist on specific standards of workmanship and expertise such as the Institute of Plumbing and National Inspection Council for Electrical Installation Contracting. These bodies supply a national list of their members, as does British Gas with its installers and fitters through the local gas showrooms or service centres.

There is also an extremely helpful organisation called The Electrical Association for Women which has at its fingertips a plethora of sound advice and information about 'all things electrical'. Here you can obtain unbiased information on how much it costs to run various appliances—like cookers, washing machines, refrigerators, and so on—and how well the various products work.

Although based in London, the EAW has branches located throughout the UK. It also organises lectures and instructive meetings all over the country and is happy to assist in any way. So if you are concerned about what you have bought or are about to buy for your new kitchen scheme, this organisation can help you.

In general, of course, the Consumers' Association will also provide invaluable advice on the choice of appliances as well as on all sorts of other products and materials as well as services.

National Home Improvement Campaign

Before you do anything positive concerning your kitchen re-plan, you must take stock of your home situation overall; it should be more than adequate. If it is not, then a lot can be done to make sure that it is, and with Government help, too.

To this end the National Home Improvement Council was set up, aimed primarily to assist people who lived in dreadful, sub-standard homes, suffering primitive conditions—like no inside toilet facilities, no baths, no hot or cold running water or unsound electrics.

Many thousands of these home owners have been able to attain a reasonable comfort level in their homes.

Now it is the aim of the NHIC to make sure that every householder should be made aware of the benefits that come from further home improvements so that any property, even though serviced with basics can achieve an even better level of comfort and eventually the long-term value of sound investment. So do not despair, what may seem like a luxury to you—from a fitted kitchen to central heating—might well prove to be well within reach.

The emphasis is on improving homes now, in every possible way and the words 'home improvement' no longer have a distasteful ring or reaction from the sources able to offer financial help.

Instead, advice as well as money is available to a number of us who may not even be aware that we qualify for it.

One cannot simply march along to the local authority offices and demand financial aid. There are, of course, provisos for the grants available as these fall into a number of categories.

Find out whether you are entitled to any of the four main House Renovation Grants, as they are called. Do this by asking for the appropriate literature from your local authority office; also for a small charge invest in a small booklet called *Improving Your Home* which is published by the NHIC and has been written in a non-complicated and lucid way for the public. Clear guide lines are given about the grants available, and suggestions on how to assess your particular needs before applying (if you qualify).

The booklet is available from the National Home Improvement Council, 26 Store Street, London WC1.

Once you have seen the literature and feel that you are entitled to one of the grants, make an application to your local authority, visit the Home Improvement Officer at the town hall and take advantage of the benefits which are by rights, yours.

Tied in with the NHIC is, of course, its membership — companies and organisations who are willing to provide practical help and free advice for you. Part of this membership list is included here (the emphasis being on those concerned in the main with kitchens).

So too, the National Federation of Builders' & Plumbers' Merchants who have a number of their own Home Improvement Centres (showrooms) scattered around the country, where one can see a wide range of equipment and materials from pipes for plumbing to kitchen cupboards in kit form. The NFBPM are also able to provide a complete list of their centres, which can be obtained by writing to: National Federation of Builders' & Plumbers' Merchants, 15 Soho Square, London W1V 5FB.

Building Centre Group

Another area from which you can get advice is through the Building Centre Group and its associates (which, incidentally, is a member of the NHIC). You can either visit them to see the permanent displays of products and materials at your disposal for any kind of home improvement project, or have literature sent direct to you through them, if you specify the type of things you are after.

Get help from

Get help from—

Consumers' Association,
14 Buckingham Street,
London WC2N 6DS
Telephone: 01-839 1222

Di Lusso Kitchens Ltd,
Orama Mill,
Hall Street,
Whitworth,
Nr. Rochdale, Lancs.
Telephone: 070-685 3991

Dunlop Floors Ltd,
10–12 King Street,
London, SW1Y 6RA
Telephone: 01-930 6700

Electrical Association for Women,
25 Foubert's Place,
London W1V 2AL
Telephone: 01-437 5212

English Rose Kitchens Ltd,
Wedgnock Lane,
Warwick
Telephone: 0926 45411

Hygena Ltd,
Charleywood Road,
Kirkby Industrial Estate,
Nr. Liverpool
Telephone: 051-548 3505

Nairn Floors Information Bureau,
Nairn Floors Ltd,
P.O. Box No. 1,
Kircaldy, KY1 2SB
Telephone: 0592-61111

Pilkington's Tiles Ltd,
P.O. Box 4,
Clifton Junction,
Manchester M27 2LF
Telephone: 061-794 2024

Solarbo Fitments Ltd,
Commerce Way,
Lancing,
Sussex BN15 8TF
Telephone 09063-63451

Wrighton International Furniture,
Billet Road,
London E17 5DW
Telephone: 01-531 7211

Get help from—

The Building Centre Group and its
   Associates,
The Building Centre,
26 Store Street,
London WC1E 7BT
Telephone: 01-637 8361

The Building Centre (Bristol),
Colston Avenue,
Bristol BS1 4TW
Telephone: Bristol (0272) 27002

The Building Centre (Cambridge),
15–16 Trumpington Street,
Cambridge CB2 1QD
Telephone: Cambridge (0223) 59625

Northern Counties Building
   Information Centre,
Green Lane,
Durham DH1 3JY
Telephone: Durham (0385) 62611

The Building Centre (Scotland),
6 Newton Terrace,
Glasgow G3 7PF
Telephone: 041-248 6212

The Building Centre (Manchester),
113–115 Portland Street,
Manchester M1 6FB
Telephone: 061-236 6933

The Building Centre (Southampton),
18–20 Cumberland Place,
Southampton SO1 2BD
Telephone: Southampton (0703)
   27350

The Engineering and Building Centre,
Broad Street,
Birmingham G1 2DB
Telephone: 021-643 1914

The Building and Design Centre,
Hope Street,
Liverpool L1 9BR
Telephone: 051-709 8484

The Midland Design and Building
   Centre,
Mansfield Road,
Nottingham NG1 3FE
Telephone: 0602-45651

The Building Information Centre,
College of Building and Commerce,
Spoke Road,
Shelton,
Stoke-on-Trent, Staffs.
Telephone: 0782-24651

Get help from some of the members of the National Home Improvement Council—

Aluminium Window Association,
26 Store Street,
London WC1E 7EL
Telephone: 01-637 3578

Association of Manufacturers of
   Domestic Electrical Appliances,
593 Hitchin Road,
Stopsley,
Luton, Beds.
Telephone: 0582-411001

Brick Development Association,
Woodside House,
Winkfield,
Windsor, Berks.
Telephone: 03447-5651

British Aluminium Co. Ltd,
Regal House,
London Road,
Twickenham, Middx.
Telephone: 01-892 4488

British Ceramic Tile Council,
Federation House,
Stoke-on-Trent ST4 2RU
Telephone: 0782-45147

Advice on ranges and installation of wall and floor tiles made by members. For complex enquiries, write to Technical Division.

British Electrotechnical Approvals
   Board for Household Equipment,
Mark House,
The Green,
9-11 Queens Road,
Walton-on-Thames, Surrey
Telephone: 98-44401

List of BEAB approved equipment which meets specific high standards of safety.

British Gas Corporation,
Domestic Operations,
326 High Holborn,
London WC1V 7BT
Telephone: 01-242 0789

Advice on gas central heating appliances, home-assembly kitchen furniture, special aids for the disabled. Tariffs and budget billing accounts. Help in obtaining hire purchase and loans. Regular schemes for central heating. Installation of products by trained fitters backed by guaranteed availability of spare parts. After sales service during the after-guarantee period.

British Gypsum Ltd,
Ferguson House,
15–17 Marylebone Road,
London NW1 5JE
Telephone: 01-486 1282

British Hardware Federation,
20 Harborne Road,
Edgbaston,
Birmingham B15 3AB
Telephone: 021-454 4385

The Building Centre Group,
26 Store Street,
London WC1E 7BT
Telephone: 01-637 1022

See separate listing of centres and associates.

Carron Company (Showroom),
48 Park Lane,
London W1Y 3LB
Telephone: 01-499 1908

Literature and advice on well-known ranges of bathroom and kitchen equipment, gas and electric cookers, radiators and heating systems.

J. A. Crabtree & Co. Ltd,
Crabtree House,
Court Parade,
Aldridge,
Walsall WS9 8LT
Telephone: 0922-53355

Delta Metal Co. Ltd,
Argyl Street,
Nechells,
Birmingham B7 5TW
Telephone: 021-328 0466

Domestic Solid Fuel Appliances
   Approvals Scheme,
Hobart House,
Grosvenor Place,
London SW1X 7AE
Telephone: 01-235 2020

Electrical Contractors' Association,
Esca House,
34 Palace Court,
Bayswater,
London W2
Telephone: 01-229 1266

Electrical Contractors' Association of
  Scotland,
23 Heriot Row,
Edinburgh, Scotland
Telephone: 031-225 7221

List of registered electrical firms.

The Electricity Council,
Marketing Department,
30 Millbank,
London SW1P 4RD
Telephone: 01-834 2333

Electricity Boards

*Information and leaflets on all types of
electrical appliances, systems, kitchen
fittings from your local Electricity
Boards' shop.*

Fibre Building Board Development
Association,
6–7 Buckingham Street,
London WC2N 6BZ
Telephone: 01-839 1122

Formica International Ltd,
De La Rue House,
84–86 Regent Street,
London W1A 1DL
Telephone: 01-734 8020

The Glass and Glazing Federation,
6 Mount Street,
London W1Y 6DY
Telephone: 01-629 8334

Glynwed. Ltd,
Headland House,
New Coventry Road,
Sheldon,
Birmingham B26 3AZ
Telephone: 021-742 2366

*Literature and information on a wide
range of products, including: Leisure
products (and a kitchen planning
service for some of the company's
units); Aga and Rayburn boilers and
cookers; Glintex u.p.v.c. window
frames; Flavel gas cookers and fires.*

Heating and Ventilating Contractors'
  Association,
34 Palace Court,
Bayswater,
London W2 4JG
Telephone: 01-229 2488

ICI Paints Division,
Wexham Road,
Slough, Bucks. SL2 5DS
Telephone: 0753-31151

*Information and literature on painting
techniques, paints, wallcoverings and
so on.*

H. & R. Johnson,
P.O. Box 1,
Tunstall,
Stoke-on-Trent ST6 4JX
Telephone: 0782-85611

*Literature and information on a wide
range of ceramic tiles for walls and
floors, as well as other ceramic
accessories.*

National Home Enlargement Bureau,
600 Kingston Road,
London SW20
Telephone: 01-542 9095

MK Electric Ltd,
Shrubbery Road,
Edmonton,
London N9 0PB
Telephone: 01-807 5151

All types of electrical accessories.

National Association of Plumbing,
   Heating & Mechanical Services
   Contractors,
6 Gate Street,
London WC2A 3AX
Telephone: 01-405 2678
Also at:
13 Newton Road,
Leeds LS7 4DL
and
Egerton House,
Wardle Road,
Rochdale, Lancs.
*List of firms who can install central
heating, modernise kitchens, etc. and
any type of dwelling.*

National Council of Building
   Materials Producers,
26 Store Street,
London WC1E 7BT
Telephone: 01-580 3344

*Advice on organisations to contact on
queries about building materials of all
kinds.*

National Federation of Builders' &
   Plumbers' Merchants
also
NFBPM Home Improvement Centres,
15 Soho Square,
London W1V 5FB
Telephone: 01-439 1753

*Their services have been mentioned in
the text.*

National Federation of Building
   Trades Employers,
82 New Cavendish Street,
London W1M 8AD
Telephone: 01-580 4041

*List of regional offices which can
supply names of firms able to carry out
home improvements.*

NEFF (UK) Ltd,
The Quadrangle,
Westmount Centre,
Uxbridge Road,
Hayes, Middx.
Telephone: 01-848 3711

Cooking equipment and appliances.

Potterton International Ltd,
Portobello Works,
Emscote Road,
Warwick CV84 5QU
Telephone: 0926-43420

Reed Building Products Ltd,
204 Great Portland Street,
London W1N 6AT
Telephone: 01-388 7631

*Literature and lists of stockists for a
number of products, including taps
and fittings, plastic pipework systems.*

T.I. Domestic Appliances Division,
Consumer Relations Department,
Radiation House,
North Circular Road,
London NW10 0JP
Telephone: 01-459 1234

*Information on gas, electric and solid
fuel domestic appliances, including
cookers, refrigeration, home laundering,
central and space heating and small
electrical appliances. The organisation
has a nationwide network of service
depots.*

Timber Research Development
   Association,
Stocking Lane,
Hughenden Valley,
High Wycombe,
Bucks. HP14 4ND
Telephone: 0240-24 3091

UBM Group Ltd,
Avon Works,
Winterstoke Road,
Bristol BS99 7PL
Telephone: 0272-664611

Institute of Plumbing,
Scottish Mutual House,
North Street,
Hornchurch,
Essex RM11 1RU
Telephone: 49-51236

Information about plumbing, generally, and a list of nationwide plumbers who belong to the institute and have to achieve a certain standard of professionalism before acceptance to the Institute's membership.

Peglars Ltd,
Belmont Works,
St Catharine Avenue,
Doncaster,
Yorkshire DN4 8DF